Texas Fish & Game's
SALTWATER STRATEGIES®
BOOK SERIES PRESENTS

PAT MURRAY'S
NO-NONSENSE GUIDE TO
COASTAL FISHING

By Pat Murray
Foreword by Doug Pike

OTHER TITLES PUBLISHED BY
TEXAS FISH & GAME PUBLISHING CO., LLC

BOOKS:

Saltwater Strategies®: Texas Reds
by Chester Moore, Jr.

Saltwater Strategies®: Texas Trout Tactics
by Chester Moore, Jr.

Freshwater Strategies:
A Practical Approach to Texas Freshwater Fishing
by Doug Pike

Texas Saltwater Classics: Fly Patterns for the Texas Coast
by Greg Berlocher

Saltwater Strategies®: Flounder Fundamentals
by Chester Moore, Jr.

Doreen's 24 Hour Eat Gas Now Café
by Reavis Z. Wortham

PERIODICALS:

Texas Fish & Game magazine (12x/year)
Texas Lakes & Bays Atlas (annual)
Texas Hunting (annual)

for information, contact us at:
1-800-750-4678
www.fishgame.com

Texas Fish & Game Publishing Co., LLC
2350 North Sam Houston Parkway East, Suite 240
Houston, Texas 77032
1-800-750-4678 • Fax: 713-227-3002

SALTWATER STRATEGIES®

PAT MURRAY'S NO-NONSENSE GUIDE TO COASTAL FISHING

By Pat Murray

Texas Fish & Game Publishing Co., L.L.C.

2350 North Sam Houston Parkway E., Suite 240
Houston, Texas 77032
1-800-750-4678
Website: www.fishgame.com

Published by

**Texas Fish & Game
Publishing Co., L.L.C.**
1745 Greens Road
Houston Texas 77032
Phone: 281-227-3001 **Fax**: 281-227-3002
Website: www.fishgame.com

Second Edition

Cover photo by Pat Murray

Foreword by Doug Pike

Production Design by Wendy Kipfmiller

Edited by Don Zaidle

ISBN: 0-929980-22-0

To Dad....life made a lot more sense
when you were here.

Contents

Foreword

When two fishermen first meet and engage in conversation, it doesn't take long for one to size up the other as either partner or potlicker. From nearly the moment I met Pat Murray, back during his previous life as a professional fishing guide, it was evident that he could fish. Not long after that, I sensed his potential as a communicator. His No-Nonsense Guide to Coastal Fishing confirms both assessments.

A diligent student to this day, Murray can be counted among those rare anglers who recognize that in terms of actually improving one's skills, there is equal reward in an empty stringer as in a full one. Rather than follow a specific method or strategy, he allows himself to be taught anew every morning by the weather and the water and the fish. And they have taught him well.

Fortunately for the redfish and speckled trout of this world, Murray is as dedicated to conservation as he is to fishing. An occasional fillet finds its way to his table, but the rest he releases for you and me.

Among the thousands of words that follow my thoughts are a number of important clues to becoming an exceptional fisherman. For those who are willing to follow it, Murray has drawn a map that leads directly to improvement and, ultimately, a greater enjoyment of your time on the water. Some of his hints will leap off the page and smack you in the face. Others lie secreted between the lines, where wise observers know instinctively to look. They are all here in one form or another, though, all the tools save rod and reel to elevate any angler's game.

Murray's work will not be the final word on the subject. No book on fishing ever was or ever could be so conclusive in a sport of infinite variables. It is, however, a solid foundation from which to build confidence in the decisions you make regarding when, where, and how to approach a day on the water.

In the hands of someone who understands and appreciates it, this is the sort of book that will be read front to back and then referenced often. In most anglers' libraries, Murray's No-Nonsense Guide to Coastal Fishing eventually will be marked by tattered edges, dog-eared pages, and scribbled notes in the margins—the ultimate tributes to a fishing book.

Doug Pike
Houston, TX

Preface

In creating a second edition of *Pat Murray's No-Nonsense Guide to Coastal Fishing*, I faced some intriguing questions of what to change in the original edition that would enhance this version of the book. One of the most common requests among readers was to add GPS numbers to the detailed bay maps. I must admit I struggled with that idea. Although I have no problem with divulging GPS numbers to any or all of the spots listed, I do not like the idea of anglers not discovering these locations with their own senses. To look at a map and find the hidden treasure is a much better experience that to look at a GPS screen and follow the track line.

Undoubtedly, GPS technology is a wonderful thing—it can actually save lives—but it also stunts the senses of budding (and experienced, for that matter) coastal anglers. An inexperienced angler with a GPS full of good numbers is like a junior shootist with a gun full of prime bullets. Just because you have an accurate gun full of top-shelf bullets does not mean you are going to shoot straight. The same is true in coastal angling. It is often better to work your way into these spots and learn the techniques of using a map and identifying landmarks, line-ups, and subsequently burning these locations into your mind. Entering coordinates and following the track line just does not have the same feeling.

As you can see, I lost on the GPS coordinate discussion. I have included the coordinates to a few key spots that consistently pay off. I do believe that the GPS numbers included in this version's maps can be of great benefit, but only when combined with the fish-finding techniques of the other chapters. Just remember to never put the spots before the basics of reading the water, carefully tracking the species you are pursuing, and finding your own pattern. Spots are just that, spots. Although often shockingly accurate, GPS numbers are merely an approximation of the spots that traditionally produce fish. These numbers will get you to the target range, but it will take focus and practice to hit the target.

The other big addition is to the Conservation chapter. Having spent the last seven years working feverishly and almost exclusively on conservation-related issues, this addition should come as no great surprise. I could write volumes on that subject alone. In this printing, I have expanded the focus of the original chapter and, hopefully, dug a little closer to the core of stewardship of our coastal resources.

The other changes may go unnoticed—a corrected typographical error or misprint—but the book remains intact and, possibly, just a bit improved.

Introduction

No secrets, no nonsense

A distinctly Texas drawl melts into the squelch of a VHF marine radio as it echoes across the bay, "Are you gettin' 'em?" It is a haunting question, resounding for all Texas anglers to answer. From the short rigs off Sabine Pass to the sprawling grass flats of Rockport, we can all answer the question. It is the point of evaluation for our angling skill. But the answer is not always pretty nor what we would like to reply.

We measure ourselves by this cruel question. Job success, financial worth, and moral strength melt away in light of this inquisition. It is not just among tournament anglers and professional fishing guides. If you "got 'em," you are a boat dock hero. You find yourself lingering around the cleaning table, repeatedly going into the marina to get a soda and asking, "How did you do today?" to anyone within earshot.

It is funny how different the scene is on a slow day. There is always a lot of talk of bad wind and no tidal movement. We tend to get very analytical about the factors that influence our fishing when things are going wrong. We all launch our boat, wade away from the shoreline, or walk out onto the jetty with great hope, but very few return with the results desired.

The No-Nonsense Guide to Coastal Fishing is a no-nonsense approach to improving your angling skills along the Texas Coast. It contains details necessary to put together the many pieces of the puzzle for successful fishing. It is never just one thing that makes a great angler. It is a combination of skills and experiences.

Going to the right spot or having a certain bait is rarely enough. You have to time your arrival, know what to look for when you get there, and select the right technique for the circumstances. You must study your surroundings and be open to new ideas, new approaches. This is part of the appeal of fishing: You are never done, never the complete angler. It requires more than simply plugging numbers into an equation that yields the right answer. It is more akin to a mystic martial art. You study, learn and improve your art. Great fishermen take it that seriously, gathering information from every conceivable source. They study fishing.

A great deal can be learned by studying the habits of great fishermen. As in any art, you start by studying "the masters." Do you suspect Mark McGwire and Sammy Sosa have studied every recorded moment of Mickey Mantle at the plate? I do. The thing to remember is that one of the fishing greats could be your best friend. He may only "get 'em" one day a year, but for that day, he is the legend. Study him. Many people spend their entire fishing life at one or two general spots and employ one or two techniques. And you know what? That is great. Fishing is many things to many people, but those who are consistently successful and produce results put no boundaries on their fishing.

Most Texas coastal anglers marvel at fishing guides. It is hard not to. The best guides seem to produce results in the face of incredible odds. As a child, I theorized about how guides spent their evenings: reading charts and reviewing old fishing texts. The reality is that they are on the phone, returning client calls and mentally sifting through the wheat and chaff of fishing reports. The fishing guide's true edge comes from fishing every day and from focus. The men and women who succeed simply try harder and want it more. Just like success in anything, it is a matter of dedication. The average angler does not have the luxury of being in touch with the day-to-day changes in the bay, but focus and desire can make up for a lot.

As a Galveston Bay fishing guide in the 1990s, I witnessed the expansion of Texas coastal angling's scope and range. This period marked the advent of modern Texas bay angling. In the early '90s, the majority of anglers—and for that matter, many guides—restricted their fishing scope to one or two local bays. You were a Trinity Bay guy or a Matagorda guy. Then freezes, floods and crowds began to move guides and anglers alike.

In the early-to-mid '90s, murmuring of East Matagorda Bay started sending anglers and some Galveston-based fishing guides to this alleged land of milk and honey. Stories of five-pound trout under staggeringly large flocks of birds and consistent limits were simply too good to be true. Surprisingly, they were not. An onslaught of guiding and fishing pressure came to this incredibly productive bay, and the eyes of the Texas angler were opened. Somehow, everyone had developed the idea it was absurd to trailer a boat for an hour or more to fish. This was no longer the case, and the Texas coast opened up.

Guides began traveling and bringing hordes of anglers with them. Sabine and Calcasuieu lakes, East and West Matagorda, Rockport and Baffin Bay were now everyday destinations. A guide's business card that once noted a bay of specialization now listed the entire coast as a range. These events ushered in the current age of great anglers. In the past, there were very few prominent anglers who received celebrity status in Texas fishing circles. There were a few guides and insiders who seemed to always catch fish, and everyone knew their names. Not surprisingly, more often than not, these guys were travelers.

Anglers like Rudy Grigar and Pete Tanner were not just fishing San Luis Pass. They were traveling from Port Mansfield to the Chandeleur Islands, and every place they went, they learned. They learned to fish over the grass of South Texas as easily as the sand and shell of Galveston. A technique or bait discovered in the marshes of Louisiana helped improve their approach on a grass flat in Port O' Connor. Fishing is fishing. All bays are connected, and all information is worthy. If you never stop studying, you never stop improving.

In preparing this book of techniques, maps, hints, and philosophies, I took into account the uncertainties inherent to the art of bay fishing. There are no guarantees. Galveston guide James Plaag put it best when asked by a client if he would guarantee a limit of trout: "I can't guarantee you that my engine is going to start tomorrow. How am I going to guarantee you a limit of trout?" Like I said, no guarantees. The rise and set of the sun is all you can count on. Tide movement, fish feeding, and wind are just a few of the uncertainties that must be dealt with each and every time your line touches the bay.

Writing this book was not unlike writing a manual on how to get struck by lightning. All you can do is run into the storm, hold your hands above your head, stand on high ground, and really want it. You can get better storm-tracking maps, better electronics to find bigger storms, and even a better lightning rod to improve your odds. But when the storm is raging, it is still unpredictable chance that gets you struck. Fishing is no different. You hone your skill, refine your focus, and increase the odds of getting struck.

When it all falls apart and you are racked with frustration, remember that you are tracking a cold-blooded animal that is expending every resource it has to elude you. This is when fishing becomes art. No longer does the modern Texas angler walk to the bank and sling out a cheese ball in hopes of a bite. The successful angler pursues his quarry, putting everything he has got into the effort.

Even as I type these words, I am studying, searching for a better lightning rod.

Chapter One

Getting the Lay of the Bay:
Philosophies for an overview of coastal bays and saltwater fishing

Getting a global view of bay systems, fish patterns, and angling techniques is the hardest part of becoming a better angler. It is so easy to become entrenched in the minutia of selecting the right lure color or learning recycled GPS numbers as though they were the secret combination to become a better fisherman. All the little details help make up the big picture, but it is often those very details that cloud our vision of the big picture and make it harder to become a better angler—the "forest for the trees" syndrome. The Zen of fishing is found in that overview or big picture of the lay of the bay and the cycles that drive it.

People will ask a consistently successful angler, "How did you know to go there at that time?" The answer is usually frustratingly cryptic: "I just had a feeling." That feeling is often what makes someone successful in whatever he or she does, but as in all pursuits, that feeling is rarely found in the little things. It is gleaned from a greater vision of all the details and an ability to connect the dots and form a picture.

There is a great expression in hunting: "Aim big, hit big." It is no different in fishing. Look at the big picture and allow your focus to expand. You will have a much greater knowledge to draw from and subsequently, a larger target for your aim.

THE LAY OF THE BAY

Many bays and bay systems are laid out in a very similar pattern. Always remember that marsh and estuary are the heart of not only the

bay system but also the larger marine ecosystem in general. Estuary areas anchor the bay and are generally in the farthest reaches of a bay complex. For example, the heart of the Galveston Bay complex comes from the Trinity River mouth, the marsh of the north shoreline of East Bay, and the limited marsh of the tertiary bays that border the west end of West Bay. These complexes of cord grass, mud pools and winding canals blend the essential nutrients from

PHOTO BY DOUG PIKE

freshwater inflow with the brine of the bay. This union creates a brackish filter for all upland elements as they enter the bay system. The marsh helps balance the salinity, creates breeding ground for the base of the bay ecosystem's feeding cycle, and creates critical habitat for everything from predators to forage species. It is the nursery.

These areas can have many variations in layout, but are always ripe with rich mud, off-color water and deep canals bordered by shallow mud flats. This is the Eden of the bay.

Visualize the body of the bay expanding from this base. Although every bay varies in specific layout, most bays and bay systems eventually empty into the Gulf. A Gulf pass is the harshest environment in this system. It is typified by strong currents, deep water, hard bottom structure, and high salinity. Passes and cuts from Gulf to bay mark the launch pad from the nest for many species, and often present a rebalancing of the food chain. An apex predator in the bay may be nothing more than an easy meal in the Gulf.

These two sides of the bay present two drastically different aspects of the bay's life cycle. The estuary is the beginning while the Gulf marks an end or passage. For a bay species, the body of the bay is the arena for the majority of its life. Almost all bay species play the careful balancing game between bay and Gulf. Many, including flounder and redfish, spawn almost exclusively in the Gulf, while trout spawn in the bay, marsh and Gulf. Yet, all three species travel the road between the two extremes in following the call to spawn and the need to pursue food.

Pelagic and semi-migratory species of the beachfront and Gulf depend on outflow from the bay to provide forage species. Without a constant cycling of menhaden, shrimp, mullet, and countless other finfish and crustaceans into the Gulf, ocean predators' buffet table would be empty. Marsh provides life to the bay; the bay funnels it to the Gulf.

Understanding this general pattern allows you to see why game fish are in certain areas at certain times of the year and, perhaps more importantly, why they are not.

Every spring, speckled trout flow into the bays to meet the early hatch of baitfish as they are flushed from marsh to the bay. Trout seek this food supply as well as look for the proper balance of salinity, current flow and protective habitat for spawning. This push from the Gulf fills the bays with schools of trout that make up the year's bay population of fish.

Fish that stream in on spring tides take up residence in the bay through summer until low tides, dropping temperatures and autumn chill purges shrimp, shad and other marsh creatures into the Gulf.

Through the year, trout generally work deeper back into the bay pursuing baitfish and seeking lower salinity. The marshes fill with fish

PHOTO BY PAT MURRAY

Sunset over the lay of the bay.

concurrently with mid-bay reefs and flats. This process concludes when the transition to fall empties a majority of the bay's biomass and resets the whole system to reload next spring. Remember, though, that these general patterns are loaded with exceptions.

After years of tagging fish for Fish Trackers Inc., I was able to find anomalies in almost every pattern. The cliché "never say never" is cliché for a reason. In the mid-1990s, I caught and tagged a 15-inch red-fish in Galveston's Green's Lake. The lake is a very small, almost isolated body of water. Although the lake has consistent numbers of large redfish in it, I believe there is a constant exchange between the bay and lake during low tides and cold conditions. I would also surmise that as redfish get to spawning size, they hear the calling to head to a pass for spawning and leave the sanctuary of the lake. I received a return on that redfish tag years later. The fish had grown to spawning size and was caught—guess where—Green's Lake. Did that fish spend its entire life in that lake? Or did it filter back and forth and get recaptured in a favorite feeding spot? It is hard to say, but it clearly indicates a repetition in redfish behavior that rivals salmon, and may show that fish are not as transient as they are sometimes thought to be.

I had a curious tag return in the early-1990s after tagging a 15-inch trout at Shell Island in the middle of Galveston's West Bay in early March. That fish was recaptured a few months later in the Gulf. Instead of coming from the marsh or the Gulf to feed on spring brown shrimp and eventually settling down to summer in the bay, I have to believe that fish never slowed down and simply followed the shrimp onto the beachfront. That gives some clue as to why West Bay fishing may be slow through the middle of summer.

The pattern of the trout in that bay may not create a substantial summer population, while the spring inflow of Gulf fish into Galveston's East Bay creates exactly the opposite result. As fish enter the

5

bay to meet the migrating "brownies" and answer the call to spawn, it sets up a substantial mid-bay reef pattern. Although completely opposite in their final results, these two patterns follow the same set of circumstances.

The most surprising tag return and pattern breaker I encountered was a trout I tagged on a beachfront pier at Freeport. It was recaptured months later from the exact same pier. I still cannot imagine that beachfront trout are not constantly on the move. Miles and miles of bars and guts, ripping tides, and large predators add up to transient fish. Either the structure of the pier pilings or coincidence found that fish sedentary in a moving environment. Anyone who has waded the surf knows that those fish are constantly on the run. This one was not.

All three of these examples show that fish are just that—fish. They are free-moving creatures that follow patterns, and part of learning those patterns is acknowledging the common breaks from the norm.

FIGHTING TRADITION

Learn the patterns, and then learn to be a rebel with a cause. Never be afraid to fish the non-traditional. In an era of seemingly limitless knowledge of bays and fish patterns, a contrary pattern can often spell success. Do not be afraid to select a spot simply to be different, or fish in adverse conditions that the average angler would shun. This is not to say you should go out in dangerous conditions or any circumstance that could risk your safety.

As a fishing guide, I was often begged to go on days that I really did not feel we would have much chance of catching anything or, for that matter, even having a pleasant trip. Sometimes anglers have so few days to fish in a year that they are determined to go anytime the chance arises, regardless of the conditions. Not surprisingly, this never-say-die attitude can help you not only find fish but also establish new patterns.

I vividly remember cowering down behind the console of my boat hiding from a 20-knots-plus northeast wind in November, trying to convince my customers to go home. My thought was that if I said it was going to be an awful day, they would believe the guide and reschedule. Their adamant desire eventually made me launch my boat and run into Galveston's West Bay to try to drift what had been some decent but not exceptional trout action under birds prior to the wind-producing front. As I rounded the protective spoil banks bordering North Deer Island, I mused that the large mass of birds in the middle of the bay looked as though they were working over fish. Clearly it had to be an aberration brought on by wind-dried eyes and my intense desire to go home. As I approached, I could see scores of other flocks dotting the horizon. The traditionally negative conditions of high wind and barometer had turned the fish on.

Oddly, that day's events turned out to be a regular pattern. Although not 100-percent accurate, I am still amazed how many days the middle of West Bay goes wide open with feeding during a cold-weather front. Possibly, it is the flush of the marsh coupled with an approaching cold night that spurs this pattern. Whatever the cause, the circumstances are not textbook, to say the least.

The Troutmasters tournament series has been a great indicator of the power of being a non-conformist. Few tournaments have been won in a crowd or, for that matter, on a "traditional" pattern. It is often the odd pattern or spot away from fishing pressure and boat traffic that wins it.

These tournaments expose a lot of great fishermen to unfamiliar settings. The interesting thing is that great fishermen will find fish even in unfamiliar settings and adverse conditions. The primary reason is that they look for fish signs and have confidence when they fish them.

With a little experience, anyone can learn to see slicks and interpret baitfish movement. There is very little to the physical act of sighting a sign. The dividing line is in interpreting and working that sign with confidence and determination.

Years ago, there was a fall tournament in Galveston that was met by a hard norther. As I was establishing my game plan for the next day, I immediately crossed out the prospects of fishing the north shoreline of East Bay. With the hard north wind and subsequent low tides, I knew from experience that wading that shoreline would be an utter waste of time. All the fish would pull off the shorelines and suspend out deep over the mud, a virtually unfishable pattern. While I wandered aimlessly around West Bay for the two days of the tournament, it was won wading the north shoreline of East Bay. Some of the tournament anglers who had caught fish on that shoreline in previous weeks ignored or were ignorant of the ramifications of low tides and off-color water and ground out their fish wading deep over barren mud. Patterns are critical, but always remember there are exceptions.

PUT IN THE HOURS

You do not learn the patterns of fish on your personal timetable. They do not feed on your schedule, so you cannot expect to catch them at a convenient time. Fish feed based on countless combinations of variables. Tide, moon, water temperature, baitfish activity, water clarity, wind, barometric pressure, salinity, cloud cover, and a host of other variables can affect feeding patterns on any given day. If your only exposure to the bay is from 5:00 A.M. until noon, you greatly reduce the odds for conditions aligning in your favor. Granted, it is hard to fish a 12 or 14 hour day, but in tough times, it can make all the difference. Remember, tenacity can often make up for lack of experience. And to gain experience, you have to be on the water.

TIDES

It is axiomatic that tide movement, velocity and direction play a significant role in the activity of all parts of bay ecosystems. From the movement of shrimp larvae deep in the marsh to trout chasing menhaden on an oyster reef, tide matters.

I admit that I have spent the majority of my fishing life trying to downplay the importance of tide movement. My point has always been that if you have a chance to go fishing, do not let sun, moon or tide stop you from going or wilt your confidence. I still believe this, but there are some simple rules that can be used to your advantage when addressing tide charts.

The closer you are to a pass, the more important tide movement is. It is very logical. In a remote back bay that gets tide movement in seasons and not hours, tide has very little effect. But for a population of fish that is congregating and feeding in close proximity to a pass or area that is subject to constant and extreme tidal movement, it is going to play into their feeding patterns.

From the broader perspective, think about how tide can move incredible numbers of fish into or out of a bay. The south shoreline of Rockport's Mesquite Bay can change dramatically in a single flood tide. As tide swells into the bay, it can bring large numbers of fish from neighboring Gulf and bay waters. The same is true in reverse. With the staggeringly quick, harsh tide drops of winter, Galveston's West Bay can go from limits of trout every day to nothing. The tide is that significant. Although these are extreme examples, they can be used to see general patterns.

As the tide falls, it pushes baitfish, game fish and everything else away from the marsh to the nearest pass. This can be exacerbated by strong winds augmenting the flow. In normal tide situations, this same pattern happens with far less extreme results. A falling tide will push fish out of bayou mouths to shorelines and off shorelines to mid-bay structure. This creates great ambush situations for anglers. When the tide rises significantly, it pushes fish onto shorelines and into back lakes and estuaries. It creates new submerged areas by flooding previously dry bay bottom. This, in turn, creates a pattern for anglers to target.

Never let tide make you cancel a trip. Use it to your advantage and ignore any bad side effects.

MOON MADNESS

Like the tide, the moon is something you will never control. You can use it to your advantage, or ignore it if it works against you. There is no doubt that a big, bright full moon allows fish to feed at night. The positive is that it also brings a decent mid-day bite and almost always creates significant tide movement. A new moon can equally create greater tide flow, but even this seemingly insurmountable tide-moving force can be overcome by a strong wind. A harsh wind can negate the strongest lunar influence.

It is natural to want to avoid full moon periods because of the increased likelihood of night feeding, but this also presents opportunity. If you are sure the fish are feeding at night, then it is a sure bet you should fish at night. Play the moon when you are scheduling a trip far in advance, but never cancel one because of the moon.

KEEP A LOG BOOK

I cannot stress enough the value of keeping a logbook. It is the single best tool to help you gain a global perspective of patterns. It allows you to look at your fishing in terms of seasons and patterns and not just trips and numbers of fish caught or not caught.

It does not need to be a blow-by-blow recap of your entire trip. Actually, that approach will likely cause you to ignore your logbook. If it mirrors the rigors of a police-style report, you will not fill it out. It should be simple and easy to complete.

List the date, locations fished (with or without success), baits used, and the key factors that influenced your catch, i.e. tide movement, wind direction and water clarity. Always leave a space for general comments or observations about your trip. Try to complete your log entries shortly after your trip. Details can fade quickly.

Even if you do not fish regularly, keep adding information to your log. Make entries based on your friends' trips. If they give you reliable information, record it. It really does not matter that you were not on the trip. When you refer back to that period in years to come, that trip may tip you off to a possible pattern that you have not tried.

READ THE NEWSPAPER

If you do not fish regularly, read the fishing reports in the newspaper. Believe it or not, the information in a major paper's outdoor report is usually reliable and accurate. Outdoor reporters are extremely particular about reports and do not want to publish false fish stories.

Although usually vague, the information is generally fresh. The key is to read between the lines. The report will never put you on "the spot" but will usually give you a general pattern. If there is a report of good numbers of fish in 5 feet of water over shell in East Matagorda Bay, you can readily establish that there are some fish on the mid-bay reefs. You may not know the specific reef that generated the report, but you have a general clue of what to look for and where to look for it.

This can work to your advantage. You do not want the newspaper to lead you in establishing a specific game plan, but it can give you the information to keep abreast of the bay and a general pattern to create a starting point.

The advent of the Internet created easy access to real-time bay conditions. There are wind and tide reports from the National Oceanographic and Atmospheric Administration websites that give almost absurd detail of tide flow velocities, wind direction and every conceivable weather-related data. There are surf cams that show beach-front conditions and buoy reports that give wave heights and swell intervals. All of this data can keep you informed about the general state of the bay and beachfront. When you are ready to go, you know more than just the current conditions. You know what the conditions have been for the past week.

Although I am sure there is some good and accurate information exchanged in fishing chat rooms, I am always suspicious of these forums. There's a reason why T-shirts silk-screened with "I fish, therefore I lie" are so popular.

THE BIG PICTURE

Having an overview of the bay, fish patterns and the conditions that drive them is critical for consistent success. I love the intensity of Bassmaster anglers. The stories of Rick Clunn camping at lakeside before a tournament to get "climatized" to the bass fascinate me. You would have to call him a nut if he did not win so many tournaments.

I would never suggest climatizing in the local marsh before your next coastal fishing trip. But when you lay out a game plan for the day, try looking with a broader vision at the climate and conditions that impact the fish. It can pay huge dividends.

Chapter Two

Getting Rigged:
Don't let your gear ruin your day

Whether you are a fisherman, hunter or gourmet chef, 90 percent of the road to success is preparation. If you do not have the proper equipment or, more commonly, too much worthless equipment, you greatly reduce your chances for a successful trip. If you are fighting your gear, you are not focused on finding and patterning fish.

From boats to fishing reels, gear selection and rigging is a highly subjective science. Everyone has an opinion on what is best. And to some degree that is a good thing. You have to select gear that is conducive to your style of fishing. Be honest with yourself about what you want out of a trip. Do not try to be the complete renaissance fisherman. If you plan to wade a bay shoreline for trout, do not go prepared to fish nearshore rigs for sharks. Instead of doing one well, you will likely do both poorly.

Try to simplify your gear wherever possible, and constantly re-evaluate your equipment. Look at each and every item you intend to

carry and ask yourself if you really need it. Try to remember the last time you used each item. If you cannot recall, it is probably extraneous and should be discarded.

Check the gear you use regularly with an eye to maintenance or replacement. Maintenance not only adds life to your equipment, it keeps you aware of its state of usability. It is much better to find out a reel is on its last legs in your garage than when you are fighting the biggest redfish of your life.

This overview touches on some of the primary considerations for optimizing your gear and, hence, improving your success as a fisherman.

BOAT RIGGING

The first thing to realize in boat ownership is that you are fighting a losing battle. By their nature, boats want to fall apart and sink. It is your goal to prevent that. Okay, I am kidding, but only a little bit. Boats require maintenance to keep them seaworthy.

Owning a boat carries with it a certain responsibility, but one that pays for itself by allowing you access to many dimensions of a coastal fishery not accessible from shore.

All boats have merit. Do not wait to get the perfect boat. As long as it is safe and seaworthy, anything is an improvement over nothing. You can always trade your way up to a bigger and more versatile boat. Many people either wait until they can afford a high-end boat, or jump into a boat that they cannot manage physically or financially.

I learned the Galveston Bay Complex in a 14-foot johnboat with a 25-horsepower Evinrude electric-start outboard. I am not saying that I would not have liked to start with a fine, fully rigged 22-foot Boston Whaler, but I might not have learned as much as I did with that starter rig. I learned the ramps because I could not run across the bay with

15

impunity. I fished backwater areas with a smaller, shallower rig. I spent more time fishing and less time running my boat.

I eventually got an 18-foot Cruiser center console with a Johnson 140 horsepower outboard. It was an ugly, yellow tub, but I swear I caught more fish out of that rig than anything I have ever owned.

Leon Napoli won the 1997 Troutmaster Amateur Angler-of-the-Year fishing primarily out of a 15-foot boat. Remember, it is not the boat that catches fish, but the angler driving it. A bad fisherman can buy the finest rig and still not catch anything. A good fisherman focuses on fishing and not what he is driving to get there.

Regardless of size, the key in rigging a boat is to create ease of operation to maximize your ability to find and catch fish. Often, it is the little things that make the most difference.

Buy a good fixed-mount compass. It's absurd to have a $30,000 boat equipped with a $5 compass. Before any electronics, buy a good compass and mount it properly on your console, ensuring that it will not become unreadable when the boat is running. It is important for learning the bay and can be the piece of equipment that will get you home in fog or storm if your GPS fails.

A depthfinder is important for both learning the bay and patterning fish. It is not a tool to keep you from running aground, but when drifting and running, it will teach you the general depths of the bay. It is indispensable when fishing mid-bay structure. Make sure your depthfinder's transducer is mounted correctly. If it does not read correctly when running at full speed, it is worthless. You need to see the bottom at all times to learn the bay.

GPS units have become so inexpensive that no boat owner has an excuse to not have one. It is important for logging fishing spots and expedient routes to them. And it can get you home in fog and storms with ease.

It is easy to ignore the details in properly rigging an anchor. When you really need to stop your boat, you had better be able to do it. When you hop out for a long wade, you do not want to have to constantly look over your shoulder just because you anchored on shell. Pick a heavy Danforth anchor and rig it with 4 to 5 feet of heavy chain. Do not make it impossible to pull up, particularly when it is buried in mud, but select something that will stop your boat.

You need a long anchor rope, particularly if you are going to fish deep areas with strong current. There is no reason to have less than 100 feet of thick rope. If stored properly, it will not be an encumbrance. Select a thick rope for ease in pulling. Remember that you or a boat mate will be pulling the anchor. Make it as easy as possible.

I have always found it best to store my anchor in a large, plastic crate-style box. You can coil the rope and chain and lay the anchor partially in the box. It allows you to keep it from tangling and can be readily moved to whatever cleat you choose.

Buy or make a good fish-measuring stick. Most anglers rely on a sticker-style measuring tape on a boat's gunwale or one on a cooler lid. Neither is reliably accurate. Either buy an aluminum measuring stick that has one end squared, or make one out of wood. Use the same device that a game warden will use when measuring fish. It allows you to push the fish's nose up against the squared side and squeeze its tail on a built-in, certified tape. You do not want to make an embarrassing, illegal (and expensive) mistake when measuring fish.

Use plenty of corrosion inhibitor. It sounds obvious, but most boat owners do not do all they can to prevent corrosion. Although there are many good brands, I always use Corrosion X. I spray it on everything from the connections in my motor to the inside of my trailer hitch. I use it on fuse panels, jack plates, trim motors, and every other moving part. It is amazing how much life it will add to everything you spray it on. If I could bath in it, I would probably live longer.

A trolling motor is clearly a luxury. They are expensive and not the most important part of your boat, but they make a tremendous difference in your ability to successfully drift-fish. From chasing slicks to working flocks of birds, a trolling motor can dramatically increase your catch. The most common mistake people make with trolling motors is mounting it on the front of the boat.

A bow-mounted motor is difficult to control; and if you fish with other anglers, it will often leave them out of the action. The motor and bracket will also take less pounding and therefore last longer mounted at the stern.

TRAILERS

Do not scrimp when buying a boat trailer. Remember that it is what holds your boat off the asphalt while you are driving 60 miles-per-hour. It gets your boat to the ramp and back home.

It should make launching one of the simplest things associated with a day on the water. If you have to fight your trailer at the ramp every trip, you either need a better drive-on trailer or need to practice. Both of these problems are solvable.

If your trailer is not easy to drive onto, look into buying a used drive-on trailer or possibly adding drive-on skids and rollers to ease the loading process. If launching and loading are too much of a nightmare, you will find yourself not wanting to go. If that is the case, a new trailer is worth the additional investment.

If you struggle due to simple lack of experience, practice. Go to an isolated boat ramp on a windy day and launch and load alone for a while. Work on it until you feel comfortable. If you can make it happen in foul weather while alone, you can launch anywhere and anytime. If you feel like a pro, you will perform like one.

A final note on trailering: Some anglers seem to never quite get the hang of backing a trailer down the ramp. The simplest way is to place your hand on the bottom of the steering wheel and watch the trailer in the rearview mirrors or through the rear windshield. As you back up with your hand on the bottom of the wheel, whichever direction you move your hand is the direction the trailer will go.

GOING BOATLESS

Although viable walk-in wading spots seem to become scarcer every year, there nonetheless remain plenty of good reasons to become proficient in the tactic.

I learned wade-fishing by walking in at the Texas City Dike and Anahuac Wildlife Refuge. I had a lot of good trips and learned a lot doing it. One of the keys to becoming adept at it is rigging correctly and not over-accessorizing. Carry the baits you are going to use, not everything you can carry. Make sure you are comfortable and do not get tired after a short wade. Have some sort of back support and a good pair of neoprene boots.

Without a boat, access is limited. Make sure you are in good enough shape to wade long distances to cover ground and find fish.

The same is true of rock-hopping jetty fishing. Your advantage on the rocks is the ability to move quickly without having to worry about anchoring. Do not ruin that edge by weighing yourself down with gear. Carry what you need and nothing more. It is enough of a task scaling rocks and trying to land fish.

Pier fishing gives you a lot more opportunity to not only carry more gear, but to employ several fishing techniques in one trip. The first thing you need is a cart. It took only a few trips to a long beachfront pier for me to see the value of a small red wagon. It doesn't have to be red, of course, but that seems to be the dominant color.

Some pier pros take the cart concept to an extreme, and if piers are your focus for fishing, it is probably a good idea. A cart enables you to carry a cooler and the rigging to fish for bull redfish and still have the equipment to toss a light spoon for Spanish mackerel. If you want to fish live bait, it is virtually impossible to walk even a short pier with a cumbersome bucket and aerator.

SELECTING WADERS

There are a few simple rules for selecting waders:

Get the lightest waders you can, and make sure they are slightly big so you can add clothing layers for cold conditions. Conversely, it is impossible to reduce the thickness of the neoprene. There are too many days along the coast that the water is too cold to wade wet, but the air is hot.

Make sure your waders snug up under your arms. You want every possible extra inch before getting wet.

Get stocking foot waders and select your own boot to fit over them. The advantages are that you will be able to change boots if you need, and you can select a boot that is more comfortable than the one that is attached to your waders. Plus, if you are wading in mud, you will not pull your foot out of a well-tied boot as easily as your foot will slip out of an attached boot. A deep-mud wade will quickly prove this advice. Last but far from least, you have the option of donning ray-proof reef boots.

Finally, try them on before you buy. It is embarrassing to stand in a store in waders, but it is worth it. Remember you will be spending a lot of time wearing them. Better to draw a few askance looks in the store than to learn out in the middle of the bay that your new waders are intolerably uncomfortable.

RODS AND REELS

Selecting the right rod and reel is critical to your success as an angler. It is like a hammer to a carpenter or a golf club to a golfer. It is the tool that makes it happen for you. If your gear is inferior, you are wasting your time. You do not have to buy a $400 rod and reel, but you should buy the best equipment you can afford. Do not expend your whole budget on ancillary items and forget about what connects you to the fish.

Always buy graphite rods. Once only for the elite, graphite rods have become very affordable. They are light and extremely sensitive. In everything from a 6-1/2-foot popping rig to a stand-up tarpon rod, graphite is the only way to go.

There are almost as many rod styles and brands as there are anglers. For general bay fishing, it is hard to beat a 6-1/2- to 7-foot short-handled, medium-light action rod. You want a utility rod with which you feel as comfortable throwing topwaters as light jigheads. Having a rod for each style of lure is great if you are a tournament bass fisherman, but it really is not applicable or necessary in saltwater bay fishing. To be honest, it is best to have your back-up rod be the exact same design and model as your primary rod. In case you have to change, you do not spend time getting the feel of a different rod.

I am a firm believer in 6-1/2-foot, short-handled rods for all lure fishing. The short rod gives you a lightning-fast hook set and better touch when finessing a bait. A medium-light action gives you enough backbone to use a large topwater without loosing the feel for ultralight baits. On the other hand, what works for me may not be comfortable for you. Go to a tackle shop or fishing trade show and try a variety of rods. If possible, hold the rod with a reel mounted on it. This will give you a feel for the balance of the rig as it will feel while fishing. A rod feels and even performs dramatically different without the weight of a reel.

For working a popping cork rig, use a 7- to 7-1/2-foot rod for enhanced casting ability with a heavy load. A medium to medium-heavy action provides more stroke to compensate for inherent slack in a popping cork rig.

Reels used to be an easy call. There were so few decent options that it was simple. Now there are dozens of domestic and foreign baitcasting and spinning reels to choose from. I believe in level-wind baitcasting reels for almost every application. They are clearly best for lures. The direct drive gives you a much better touch on your lure than the slack of a spinning reel. Once mastered, they do not produce the tangles and line twist inherent to spinning reels, and under some conditions, can cast farther.

I have fished with a number of great lure and bait fishermen who swore by spinning equipment. You have to decide what you like, but make sure you try both options before making a choice.

Technology has advanced to the point that almost any $100-range reel has an adequate drag system. I use Shimano reels almost exclusively. They have a great selection of price ranges, and even the lower-end models perform better than the top-flight stuff from just a few years ago.

In choosing a line for bay fishing, do not go any lower than 12-pound-test. If you fish around any structure at all (which you will), you need more abrasion protection than lighter lines provide. On the flip side, most lines heavier than 15-pound test increase visibility to spooky fish and reduce casting range.

Although I know countless anglers who use a leader, I do not. That puts me firmly in the minority. Most saltwater anglers are possessed with a shock-leader fetish. My thinking is that I want nothing that will change the action or appearance of my bait. With the advent of fluorocarbon line, I am rapidly running out of excuses, but for the time being, I am standing my ground.

I equally do not like snaps or snap swivels. I use a small swivel on spoons, but otherwise, I prefer to go nude, even with twist-prone jerkbaits. Mickey Eastman once told me, "Snap swivels are kinda like a booger hanging off your bait." I have to agree.

I use one knot. I am not saying that is right, but I have tried a lot of different knots and keep using the improved clinch knot. If I used a leader, I would use a blood knot. I tie direct to every bait and use a split ring as opposed to a loop knot on topwaters. I am a grumpy man, and I like it that way. Being a curmudgeon in certain areas has its advantages.

ROD AND REEL MAINTENANCE

When cleaning rods and reels, less is more. The temptation is to coat everything in heavy oil. Considering the corrosive nature of saltwater, the tendency to over-oil is understandable, but rinsing rods with fresh water after every trip is often plenty of maintenance. Periodically check the rod eyes for rust, and clean the reel seat so salt does not build up.

If possible, clean your reels after every trip. It does not take a complete break down, simply wipe off the reel. Never spray it down with a high-pressure hose. That will only drive grime and sediment into hard-to-reach crevices and corners. Apply light oil on all external moving parts. Take off the side plate and wipe out the interior to remove excess oil and any water. It takes only a small amount of oil to lubricate a reel. Excess will only become an attractant for dirt and salt.

After every third or fourth trip, clean the drag system and use a small amount of drag grease to re-lubricate it. If your reel is starting to grind, you have waited too long to clean it. Try to stay out front with maintenance, and your reels will last a lot longer.

FIRST AID KIT

I feel like my mother for writing this section, but a first aid kit can be an incredibly valuable thing—perhaps even life-saving. You do not have to get the most expensive African Safari Survival Kit. Purchase a basic marine medical kit that has adhesive bandages, anti-bacterial cream, a hook-removal kit, antiseptic, aspirin, gauze wrap and pads, adhesive tape, scissors, and other odds and ends for dealing with common first aid situations.

Failure to treat what may at first appear to be a slight wound can lead to serious problems later due to infection. A jab from a fin or cut from a gill plate can "inject" pathogens directly into the wound. Immediate cleansing with antiseptic, a dab of anti-bacterial cream and bandage covering can spell the difference between temporary discomfort and a throbbing, swollen appendage later on. Get a kit, and use it as needed.

Chapter Three

Fish Signs:
The fundamentals of fishing

Fish signs are the most important element in the art and science of locating fish. Without signs, we are merely guessing. Unfortunately, the fish do not always give us the luxury of a flashing neon "Fish Here" sign. It is often a subtle swirl or smeared slick that present the clue. Like a good detective, the best fishermen look for the clues and put together a pattern to catch their quarry. They use the fundamentals of fishing to their advantage.

READING SLICKS

Many coastal fishermen fear slicks. They are critical to successful wade- and drift-fishing, yet many anglers do not have a clear idea of what a slick is or how to locate one.

What is a slick? It is the oily regurgitation of a fish. The slick creates an oil spot on the surface of the water and usually a sweet smell similar to watermelon or fresh-cut grass. It is generally small at first and gradually expands under the influence of wind and current.

A big slick is not necessarily a bad thing. It tells you that there are fish in the area and can sometimes result from many smaller slicks blending into a large one.

Not all slicks create the same sheen on the water. What has been regurgitated significantly impacts the appearance of the oil. When fish are feeding on shad, there is a pronounced oil spot. When they are feeding on crabs and shrimp, there is less oil and often less slick. Be observant. Slicks do not always reach out and flash "Fish Here."

Believe it or not, many species other than specks and reds slick. Flounder, gafftopsail catfish, hardhead catfish, Spanish mackerel, sand trout, bluefish, and any other predator species can slick. As always, any slick is good as signs go. Even if it is not produced by your target species, it indicates feeding activity in the area and therefore, the presence of feeding fish. If your target species is in the area, it is likely feeding, too, or soon will be.

Working slicks requires patience. They are not a guarantee but an important part of the equation to catching fish. A slick does not necessarily mean the fish that produced it are feeding or are directly under it.

Fish can slick when they are frightened or have finished feeding. It is not unusual for fish to start slicking after a binge feed. You may notice that the slicking starts after you have quit getting bites. This is important to remember when fish are slicking all around you yet you cannot catch anything. It may be a simple timing issue. The one incontrovertible fact about a slick is that outside of a crab trap or petroleum spill, a slick tells you that there are fish in the area.

MUD BOILS

Bent rod...big smile.

A mud boil is an off-color cloud of silt or mud stirred up by a bottom-rooting or startled fish or school of fish. They are generally associated with redfish and drum. Both species have an affinity for rooting in mud for burrowing crabs, shrimp and sand worms.

Remember that several other species can create mud boils. I have been shocked a few times after working boils that turned out to be made by gafftopsail catfish—a very disappointing surprise. The flip side is that other more desirable species often lurk behind mudding fish and pick up what they scare off the bottom.

I once cleaned a 5-pound trout that had been caught in the middle of a school of mudding redfish in Galveston's Christmas Bay. Its stomach was unusually distended, and upon opening it, I found an undigested half of a large blue crab. It had been crushed in half, and I imagine swirled away from the feeding pack of redfish in the melee. The trout swept in and swallowed the flashing crab half. Clearly an uncharacteristic meal for a trout, but a great indicator of a pattern behind mudding fish. That trout was waiting in ambush for anything kicked up from the mud.

Mud boils can be very difficult to see. Even to the most experienced angler, a mud boil can go undetected. The best way to get better is to practice looking for them. Watch when anything creates mud, and

take a moment to study it. Even the drag of a shrimp trawl will help you become accustomed to looking for this type of discoloration. During a wade, kick up some mud and look at the way the cloud blooms and settles. It will help you learn what to look for and to "age" the cloud by observing the rate of decay.

Big red, bigger smile.

READING BIRDS

The presence of birds always means something. From the heron on the bank to the sharp-eyed tern, birds always indicate baitfish.

The application of birds as fish signs vary. The most common bird sign is a flock of gulls or terns hovering over shrimp or shad driven to the surface by a school of predator fish. As with most signs, the birds may not always be over the species you are targeting. It is possible to encounter everything from speckled trout to croaker chasing baitfish under birds.

Gulls and terns are opportunists and are not always working over fish. They can gang up over a dead fish, trash, a worm hatch, and, curiously, ducks. Diver ducks kick up all sorts of bottom-dwelling creatures as they feed, and gulls hover over them trying to pick up leftovers or steal anything they can. It is extremely difficult to tell that gulls are over ducks until you are right on top of them. Even that harbors a lesson for the observant angler: Check out every flock, even if you are sometimes disappointed by what you discover. It pays off more often than not.

Terns are often referred to as "liar birds," an unfortunate misnomer. Liar birds are anything but deceptive. They are almost always over minnows or small shad and, commonly, over feeding fish. Granted, there are times when you cannot catch a thing under a flock of terns picking away at micro-small baitfish or banging away at a tide line or rip, but they can be a great signal of baitfish during winter, when signs are at a premium.

Terns generally have better eyesight than gulls. The next time you work a flock of mixed gulls and terns, watch how the terns see the shrimp or shad before the gulls. You will even see gulls key off terns. The terns will be the first in the pack to make a move.

Terns often find a baitfish school first, and gulls pile in behind. This can be critically important when you are trying to track a school of fish that are pushing up very small or few shrimp. You can hang back and watch the terns to decide your next move to intersect the school without inadvertently running through them.

As hated as cormorants are on inland lakes and fish farms, they are of great value when looking for baitfish during winter. There are times when they are the only baitfish indicators you will get. They cruise the bay, submerging to catch minnows and small baitfish. When signs are scarce, they can provide the only clue to pattern a drift or build confidence for a wade.

A lurking group of pelicans cruising the bay can be a great indicator of baitfish. They paddle along and crunch their necks to reduce their profile. When they spot a mullet, the neck unfolds to launch the beak at the baitfish. When you see a pack of pelicans cruising a cold winter shoreline, it may be as solid a "Fish Here" sign as you could desire.

COLOR CHANGES AND LINES

A lot of things can create color changes and color lines in the bay and nearshore waters. Strong tides, rooting fish and stirring baitfish can all create visible color changes. Although all three of these scenarios are drastically different in origin, they all create a contrast of water clarity that, in turn, creates a form of secondary structure. This contrast is a murky camouflage for baitfish and an ambush point for predators. Color lines can be the meaningless result of a dirty tide rolling in or turbidity formed as water turns over and muddies. Nonetheless, all color lines should be explored. In the absence of other signs, they make a good starting point for waders and drifters alike.

BAITFISH ACTIVITY

Not enough can be written or said about the value of baitfish. Looking for trout, redfish or anything else in an area barren of baitfish is like looking for swans in the desert. No bait means no fish. On the other hand, what do you do when the entire bay seems carpeted with mullet? A great excuse for not catching anything that many use (myself included) is citing too much bait in the water. What does that mean? Too many targets? Maybe, but in this situation the subtle art of interpreting the actions of baitfish comes into play.

Mullet, shad and minnows all exhibit flight responses to predators. Even in a seemingly endless carpet of mullet, you can see the playful jumps of mullet turn to scurried darts. It is funny that there is too much bait in the water only when we do not catch anything. There are countless times when an erratic topwater is met with staggering blow-ups even in a crowd of seemingly sedate mullet.

A keeper.

PHOTO BY PAT MURRAY

Quick bites under a flock of birds.

PHOTO BY DOUG PIKE

SIGNS IN GENERAL

Fish signs provide our greatest tools for locating and tracking game fish. They are often subtle and rarely static. Feeding fish are often moving, and their signs are like the tracks of a deer. You always have to look farther ahead on the trail to intercept them.

Never ignore any clue. Discount it and move on, but do not ignore it. They come in many forms, some more cryptic than others, but when tracking a cold-blooded animal in what is actually a trackless environment, take every sign with gratitude and use it to your advantage.

Chapter Four

Drift Fishing Tactics:
Overcoming drift fishing intimidation,
what to look for and how to capitalize on it

CATCH THE DRIFT

There are very few great drift-fishermen. Drifting is arguably the worst part of most bay anglers' game. It sounds strange. Logically, drift-fishing should be simple. You stop your boat, drift and cast. Unfortunately, it is one of the hardest parts of successful bay angling yet one of the most important.

The farther north and east you are on the Gulf coast, the more critical drift-fishing becomes. Although drifting can be a key

The redfish is oversized…the cigar is in the slot.

33

tool in South Texas, from the Colorado River north, it is crucial. The generally steep shorelines and deep mid-bay structure of Matagorda, Galveston and Sabine make it an inescapable reality of successful fishing.

Learning to drift-fish successfully is not easy or always fun. It is like trying to make yourself go to the gym and work out. You want the body, but you feel like you are missing all the fun as you labor through the education and building process. You would like the muscles and all the perceived perks that go with them, but the investment of time, effort and sweat seem too high a price.

Learning to drift takes dedication. If you learn to be an effective fisherman out of a boat, you are ahead of literally 95 percent of the entire Texas coastal fishing public. To be honest, you are ahead of the majority of professional guides.

Effective drift-fishing is what separates the great from the weak in guiding, tournament fishing and weekend angling. It adds a key dimension that is missed by most fishermen. Even among the diehard drifters who fill mid-bay reefs and well pads every summer weekend, few excel at it and maximize their catching potential. It is an underutilized technique. If you want to find secret spots in overcrowded bay systems, the best secrets of all may be in the middle of the bay.

Think about any bay system, particularly the deeper bays of the upper coast. Wadeable shorelines and reefs are a minor portion of the total bay acreage. Granted, shorelines are a key piece of habitat for almost all baitfish and game species, but speckled trout to a large degree and redfish to a lesser degree spend more time away from shorelines. The key to catching these fish is learning the bottom structure, signs to look for, techniques to use, and the confidence to stick with it.

The final component to successful drifting is being aggressive. I do not mean behavior that would incite "bay rage" but a focus and drive to actively pursue fish from a boat. Boat fishing is often associated with lazy and simple fishing. It is actually the opposite. To be consistently successful while drifting, you have to constantly look for signs and always plot your next move. You have to be alert to your surroundings and capitalize on the smallest clues to where the fish might be. A good drift-fisherman is always working, pushing the tempo of his or her fishing.

LEARNING THE BOTTOM

Learning to drift-fish is a building process. To build the foundation, you have to learn the bottom of the bay. Texas bays have a wide variety of bottom structures. With grass, oyster shell, clam or mussel shell, channels, bottom contours, sand, mud and rock, Texas drift-fishermen have a lot of targets. Almost all of these structure types help attract baitfish by providing protection from predators, a break from current and a surface for algal growth. Anglers must learn to locate, identify, read, and fish each bottom type.

Before addressing any structure, you must have the tools to find and interpret it. This is the first and hardest hurdle on your way to mastering not only drift-fishing but all other fishing techniques. Outside of fishing grass beds, you are generally floating over water that is somewhat murky. You cannot really see or feel the bottom. It is often tough to know where your lure or bait is in the water column or if you are really on fish habitat at all. It can be disquieting, and is the leading reason most people give up trying to improve their drifting skills.

Most bay anglers have never consistently put together good catches of trout and redfish unless there was a flock of birds guiding the way, or they were fishing visible structure with live bait. The drawback of both of those patterns is that everyone else on the bay stands just as good a chance of seeing that wheeling pack of birds or production platform as you do. Learning to fish the subtleties of the bay bottom will set you apart from the crowd, literally and figuratively. You will have to ignore the feeling that you are not in the right place or that you do not know how to read the signs. You have to use "the force" (focus and have confidence), and always remember that even if you are not catching fish at that moment—or even on that trip, you are learning the bay.

THE DIGITAL DEPTHFINDER

A good depthfinder is the first and most important tool you will need to learn the bay bottom. Do not confuse the term "good" with "expensive." You do not need a color screen, 3000-foot range machine. Actually, simple is better. You need a digital depth display with some rudimentary bottom-charting capabilities. Make sure it will display depth while you are running. You will be surprised how many ledges and humps you find as you run across a bay.

PHOTO BY PAT MURRAY

Remember that the bay bottom is not static. It changes with tide and the impact of man. Although at times destructive, a small dredging project can create bay bottom structure overnight that may remain for years. A good depthfinder will reveal this "new world" to you.

Charting capabili-

A successful drift: note the slicks off the bow.

ties can be helpful when fishing defined drops and ledges. The bottom line on the chart can help you visualize the slope you are fishing. It is also useful for discovering schools of suspended baitfish, both in the bays and near shore. When tarpon fishing, a good chart can help find the schools of menhaden that can define a pattern for the entire season.

Knowing depth is vital while drifting, whether it is a deep reef or shallow grass bed. Fish will suspend at a certain depth due to temperature, structure change or tide flow. As you drift, you may catch trout along the taper of a reef that breaks from shell to mud. It may involve only a small depth change but can mean the difference between getting bites or not. As you watch your depthfinder and compare the various depths to the success of a given drift, it can set a pattern for the day and even establish a pattern that remains consistent for years.

When you are on a school of fish that you located under feeding birds or slicks, note the depth. There is always a reason why fish appear in a given spot. Even if they are simply following a school of shrimp or shad, the fact that those fish are there and feeding tells you it is a good ambush spot that could pay off in various conditions.

THE MANUAL DEPTHFINDER

The quickest way to become a great drift-fisherman is to use a 10-foot piece of PVC pipe. Amazingly, this marvel of modern technology transcends the touch of the most sophisticated gray-line indicator. A probing length of pipe can give you an accurate read of depth and exact feel for bottom texture, helping form an accurate mental image of the bay bottom. When learning to fish submerged mid-bay reefs, the pole will teach you the subtle structure transitions that make up a reef and, more importantly, make for a good drift. It is these subtleties of structure that hold fish the majority of time.

With the touch of the pole, you can essentially walk the bottom in areas too deep to wade. A successful wade-fisherman is always feeling the bottom with his feet, sensing for structure transitions. A great drifter should be no different. As with a digital depthfinder, the time to really pay attention to bottom details is when you are actively catching fish. Even if you stop on a flock of birds working over trout in the "no man's land" of an open bay, take time to feel the bottom. You may find a reef or hard spot in a desert of mud. This is how secret spots are discovered.

When you are catching fish on a known reef, probe the bottom where you are getting bites. You may find a taper, ridge or mud spot that consistently holds fish. If you found the school because of a slick or bird, the next time you come back to it you may be able to catch fish without needing to depend on signs. Not surprisingly, that spot will likely continue to hold fish.

Although you may look and feel like a complete loser jabbing around in what to observers is obviously deep water, you are learning hidden secrets that will set you apart from the crowd.

GETTING BACK TO YOUR SPOT

There are many uses for a Global Positioning System (GPS) unit. Key among them is the ability to relocate obscure bits of structure. Dismantled oil and gas production platforms leave a ghost of structure when they are gone. These oyster shell pads continue to attract bait and game fish long after the rig is gone. Without visual lineup references, these reefs are nearly impossible to find. A GPS unit changes all that by recording and storing location coordinates of your favorite places and the most expedient routes to them.

When probing the bay bottom, you can record all the shell structure you find but merely recording your spots on the GPS is not enough. As a backup, record in a ledger or fishing diary all the spots stored in the GPS. GPS units do get smashed or stolen and are not immune to malfunction.

Further, draw small, detailed representations of the spots you have recorded. Create an image of the bay bottom and an overhead of where it is located in the bay. This will help you put together a mental and physical map of the bay. By visualizing the bay structure, you carry a mental picture of the spots you fish.

TALK TO A SHRIMPER

I credit Capt. David Wright, longtime Galveston Bay guide, with the sage observation, "If you want to know where the trout are, ask a shrimper." Where there are shrimp, there are trout. A shrimper has a keen understanding of the migratory patterns of white and brown shrimp and, more importantly, knows what stage of a pattern they are in at any given time. Their livelihood depends on it. Many of the inter-bay migratory patterns of trout follow those of shrimp. Outside of spawning, few factors are more influential on trout movement than shrimp migration. If you understand shrimp-movement patterns, you understand trout-movement patterns.

This is not to say you want to follow shrimpers around to pick a pattern, but the movement of shrimp boats is a great indicator of shrimp movements.

Although there can be great variation due to rain and other cyclical conditions, brown shrimp leave the marsh in-mass during spring. Not surprisingly, flocks of birds dog shrimp already beleaguered by schools of trout and redfish. This spring pattern plays out along the entire coast, generally beginning first in the bays of South Texas, then gradually moving north and east up the coast as waters warm. The combination of warming water and changing seasons brings on this perennial event. In fall, the exit of the white shrimp can bring dramatic fishing results. You can watch the shrimpers move from bay to channel as herds of shrimp move from the marsh on their trek to the Gulf.

Most shrimpers know more about a shrimp than you or I would ever care to know, but a little update now and then can help expand your insight into the current pattern of this much-desired crustacean.

AN OYSTER BOAT CAN BE YOUR FRIEND

Generally associated with noisy shell dredging and dirty water, oyster boats are often considered a plague on bay reefs. Their cumbersome dredges rake the reef for oysters, creating grinding noise and

PHOTO BY PAT MURRAY

A mud boil black drum: note the large redfish that followed the drum to the surface.

clouds of sediment. These are usually not good conditions for fishing, but do not give up too soon. In the 1980s, many days in Galveston's West Bay were focused around drifting the edges of dredge clouds carried away by current and wind. The usually clear water became clouded with silt and, more importantly, bits of oyster and crustaceans crushed in the shelling and dredging process. This serendipitous chum line attracted baitfish, plus created synthetic ambush points for opportunistic trout and redfish. Sharp drift-fishermen capitalized on the scenario to score big.

Oystering practices have changed in West Bay, but there are still opportunities to utilize this pattern throughout coastal bays. It is not a sure bet. Often, the noise and turbidity are enough to drive away fish and fishermen alike. Nonetheless, a small pack of oyster boats are often worth a try, particularly when targeting redfish. I have actually seen redfish action on a reef dissipate when the oyster boats left. It is easy to surmise that the absence of pre-ground oyster prompted the reds to leave.

Just as a shrimper knows shrimp, an oysterman knows shell. By carefully watching oyster boat movements, you can learn the dimensions of a reef, the portions that have live shell, and occasionally, the location of an unknown reef. If an oyster boat is dancing its telltale dredge swing, it is a sure bet there is shell there. Even if you cannot fish that spot that day, a quick input into your GPS stores the location for future probing.

EVEN CRABBERS CAN HELP

Although an obscure hint to changing bay patterns, a crabber's daily rounds exposes crab movements. This can be a great indicator for locating redfish concentrations. Crabbers naturally place traps in areas where they get the best results. A vague sign, to be sure, and just one element in establishing a pattern.

One seldom-acknowledged benefit to watching crabbers is their arguably peerless knowledge of the bay. They generally know the quickest way to get from point A to B and know every obstruction along the way. Their traps track some of the lesser-known and obscure paths through the reefs and obstructions of a bay. Be careful, though. Some crabbers use jet-drive boats and run traps in water so thin it is accessible only by air or jet-drive boat.

THE VALUE OF VISION

Your eyes are the best tool available for consistently finding fish.

This is never more true than when drift-fishing. The best way to improve you bay vision is with a quality pair of polarized glasses. It never ceases to amaze me when fishermen will have a $500 rod and reel and $5 no-name glasses. Spending $100 or $150 on a quality pair of glasses opens up a whole new visual world, enabling better penetration beneath the water, reducing glare and keeping your eyes sharp for longer periods without fatigue.

Pick glasses that are comfortable and suited to your style of fishing. Make sure the frames are light. Heavy frames are fatiguing during an all-day grind on the bay. You want a tight fit to reduce glare entering from the sides and to block wind from drying your eyes. I have found a slight wrap-around style works best. Try several styles to find the frame best suited to the shape of your face. Remember, for glasses to augment your vision and improve your fishing, they must be comfortable.

There are three basic lens colors: gray, amber and vermilion. Each has its strengths and weaknesses. Gray is the most soothing lens. It cuts glare and gives the water surface a "dull finish" look. It is great when looking for surface-oriented signs (slicks, birds and baitfish) with a high sun but has very little surface penetration.

Amber or yellow has less glare-cutting qualities but provides superior water penetration over gray. It also aids low-light vision.

Vermilion or red is the brightest lens. It is best in low-light situations or when water penetration is crucial. When sight casting to fish or other specific targets (e.g. sand holes in a grass flat), vermilion is unbeatable.

No lens choice is wrong, but try to find the combination of lens and frame that makes you the most comfortable and confident. Your sunglasses are your window to the signs that lead to fish. Do not cut corners on this purchase.

SIGNS BEYOND THE OBVIOUS

Finding a slick, mud boil or flock of birds is important, but without the ability to read and interpret these signs, they are meaningless. Simply seeing a slick or mud boil does not spell instant success. Sometimes a sign only tells you fish were there. The trick is to find where they are now.

SLICKS

Fishing slicks is one of the key patterns for spring and summer drift-fishing. When filled with summer schools of trout, reds and every other finfish, mid-bay reefs and spoil banks are often covered with slicks. Anyone who has spent time fishing slicks has had some frustrating experiences trying to get bites in what appears to be a feeding frenzy. As mentioned in Chapter 3, slicks do not always indicate feeding activity. This is often the case when drifting hot water. You may be on the school, but they are simply coughing up what they ate earlier. The silver lining is that you have found fish. If you stay with them, you can pry out a few fish until they feed again.

When looking for slicks, increase your range of vision by standing on your console seat or the console itself. The added elevation increases your vision dramatically.

Sometimes slicks appear as one big blob covering a large portion of the water surface. From years of brainwashing, people tend to ignore large slicks. The overlooked reality is that a huge slick may actually be a lot of little slicks. Do not ignore a slick just because it is big. It is important to approach this sign from upwind and upcurrent if possible, and watch for a pattern in the slick. Look for smaller slicks around the edges of the large one or trails of slicks extending out from the blob. This "tracking" is the best way to target a moving school. Fish will slick while moving and, not unlike hunting on land, give you a track or trail to follow. You must use your trolling motor or idle your boat to get in front of these tracks. It is rarely easy. You may have to follow a school for some time before getting in proper position to fish. When the slicks pop, try to anticipate where the next one will come up, and position yourself to intercept.

Sometimes slicking fish are not the species you are looking for. When following slick trails, you may find gafftopsail catfish at the head of the school and trout at the rear. The most important thing is to interpret where the slick came from and where the school that made it is going.

Slick fishing can be frustrating at times. Once you see a slick, the rest should be easy, right? It rarely is. In any given day of slick fishing, there are going to be some duds. These duds may have been from good schools that you missed connecting with due to wind or current. Possibly, that school was not feeding, or you just simply did not get a bite.

There are always a few mystery slicks that you would swear were real until you race across the reef only to find it is foam or nothing at all. This is all part of the game.

Finding a slick is only the first piece of the puzzle. The real key to success is staying with the pattern. The more you track slicks, the better you will get at interpreting them. Some of the best fishing in a bay is over-looked or ignored because of angler uncertainty at reading slicks or the inevitable frustration when the pattern does not produce immediately.

Sometimes when your slick pattern disappears, you can resort to the unthinkable and try to spook the school. Anglers devote a great deal of attention to not spooking fish. However, when you lose the track of the school, or it simply quits producing slicks, firing up your outboard may produce a spook slick that puts you back on them or gets them moving again. This is an unconventional method, but is surprisingly effective.

Another ploy is driving a short circle around the area where you think the fish are. This motion may enable you to see another group of fish if it does not incite the one you were pursuing. As an aside, I do not recommend doing this on a crowded reef unless you want to learn the true meaning of "bay rage."

MUD BOILS

Mud boils are probably the hardest fish sign to find. Getting on a mud boil pattern is often a matter of accident. Commonly, redfish rooting around the edge of a reef or across a mud flat produce a slick.

When flounder migrate, the results can be phenomenal.

PHOTO BY PAT MURRAY

As you approach the slick, the mud boils become more obvious.

Not unlike slicks, the key to fishing mud boils is interpreting the pattern. The fish are moving as they feed, rooting in the mud, and often ignore anything not literally under their noses. You can track mudding fish for long period without a bite, then suddenly have everyone in the boat hooked up at once. You must be patient and watch for new mud boils all the time.

A trolling motor is mandatory equipment for fishing mud boils. These fish often spook easily, and a trolling motor will allow you to get properly positioned without alerting them.

It is very easy to lose the track of mudding fish. Commonly, redfish and drum will mud for a period, then suddenly stop. You may even lose the school in the mud they have already produced. This is the time to try to spook the school. Race your engine and immediately shut it off. The blast of commotion will make the school spook and kick up a fresh boil. You can then relocate them and start tracking again.

You can also try sending a lookout up into the "crows nest" atop the console and make a short run around the area the fish have been tracking. The lookout will be able to see the general trend of the school's movement and possibly locate another school or splinter group of the original school.

Remember that these fish are rooting for food. It is often advisable to fish a jig slowly on the bottom mud. If the school is doing more rooting than feeding, this will sometimes elicit a bite.

BIRDS

Fishing under birds is arguably one of the most exciting brands of drift-fishing. Although the feathered fish finders may be working over bluefish, sand trout, ducks, or a host of other unwanted targets, a flock of wheeling birds will jumpstart the heart of the most callused of bay anglers.

The technique seems simple enough: See a flock, pull within casting range, and hook up. If only it was that easy. Sometimes it is, but not always. When birds are vigorously working over schools of trout, it is as close to a slam dunk as you will get on the bay. Even when things are working out just right, there are subtleties that can maximize your catch.

The most important tool for bird fishing is a good pair of binoculars. As with sunglasses, you need a quality pair. There are a surprising number of affordable waterproof, perma-focus binoculars on the market. Remember that these glasses will likely not receive the best of care and will be subject to no small amount of abuse. You will probably store them in a dry box or cooler. They will be exposed to salt spray and get bumped around on your console or deck when you race from flock to flock. Look to strike a balance between serviceability, ruggedness and cost.

Good lenses enable you to see flocks of birds from incredible distances. As you scan the horizon, with or without binoculars, look for the white and black flashes of gull and tern wings. Sometimes you can see the flashes before you see the flock.

When running the bay looking for flocks, do not climb up on your seat or console. Unlike when looking for slicks and mud, additional elevation actually works against you when pursuing birds. You want to get as low as possible to distinguish birds from the horizon. The more you can look up and see the flock against the blue of the sky, the easier it will be to see a subtle flash.

A trolling motor is a must for successful bird fishing. Although there are times when you can "Rambo" a flock by plowing into them and still produce fish, the majority of time a quiet approach produces more fish.

It is difficult to give a definitive distance to stop your boat when working birds. You have to consider the influence of wind pushing your boat and the speed of the school the birds are following. The best approach is a cautious one. Stop upwind and observe what the flock is doing. Are they having trouble staying on the school? Are they moving fast to keep up? These distinctions can make all the difference in catching one fish or many per flock.

Try to read where the head of the school is. The birds will rush to grab a shrimp or shad that is being pushed ahead of the school. Once you determine the direction of movement, troll out in front and intercept the school.

If the school under the birds is very small, very fast or extremely skittish, your trolling motor works against you. This is when the "Rambo" method comes into play. Run your boat wide open until you are almost under the flock. Cut the engine, spin the steering wheel to turn the boat broad side, and grab your rod and start casting. It can be very exciting, productive—and dangerous. The boat will usually rock and pitch for several seconds and can easily sling an unsuspecting angler overboard. (Trust me, I have seen it happen.)

As you may imagine, it does not take too many "Rambos" to kill bird action. Surprisingly, though, when the fish are feeding aggressively and the bird action is hot, you can crash a flock, and it will spring back up immediately.

PHOTO BY PAT MURRAY

You are never too young to catch a redfish.

COLOR CHANGES

Reading a color line is similar to interpreting slicks. Although a smaller color change or color streak is most desirable, a large color change or line can be fished successful-ly. Always look for the subtle, smaller components of the larger sign.

As you approach a color line or streak, look for fingers of cloudy water and breaks in the color line that will serve as an ambush point for a predator. These nuances can hold and concentrate fish that move along the larger structure of the color change. Although working a color change can be as simple as drifting to the edge and getting bites, it often takes a keen eye to capitalize on this transient structure.

The general thinking in fishing a color change is that baitfish and predators are going to be directly along the color change edge. Not necessarily. It is not uncommon to find trout and redfish far from the color change itself. It is equally common to find them in the middle of the color blob. The key is to thoroughly fish all sides of the color change and the outside perimeter before giving up on it.

BAITFISH

Active baitfish are the Alpha and Omega of fish signs. It does not matter if you are on Galveston Bay or Lake Guatemala, nervous baitfish indicate active predator fish.

When mullet and shad carpet the beachfront and surface of the bay, it is difficult to distinguish a meaningful school of baitfish from the mysterious jumping antics of mullet. There is no easy answer. Targeting active baitfish can result in incredible action but can also leave you frus-trated. Baitfish are an important part of the puzzle but not the whole picture. At the very least, active bait gives you a solid starting point from which to locate other indicators of game fish.

MAXIMIZING YOUR CATCH

Even when you locate the fish, correctly read the signs, and start catching fish, there is more you can do to maximize your catch.

Granted, once you are getting bites, the majority of the battle is won, but there are tactics that can turn a five-fish drift into a fifty-fish drift.

Carry a drift marker. A small, brightly-colored buoy tossed overboard where you find fish provides a target to fine-tune a drift. All schools are not sedentary enough to mark this way, but when you catch several fish in one area, throw your marker. It does not always work, but on a slow-bite day and particularly during winter, it can make a big difference. If you continue to get bites on repeated drifts, you can concentrate your efforts to try to maximize your catch from that school by trying different baits and retrieves.

A drift marker also gives an indication of how you are drifting. It is easy to account only for the influence of wind on your drift. A fixed marker shows how all influences—wind and current—are affecting your drift. It helps you line up accordingly and maximize the amount of time in the "red zone."

Odd as it sounds, an anchor can make or break a drift-fishing trip. It is easy to find yourself making long drifts but only catching fish in a small area or even working slicks that seem to appear from the same general spot. These are signs that the fish are tight to some form of structure and can be better targeted from an anchored boat. If you drop a marker on a school of fish and are successful on several drifts, try anchoring just short of the marker on the upwind or upcurrent side. The same procedure can work when fishing slicks. If the wind and current allow, try to anchor off the side rather than the bow of the boat. This will hold the boat broadside to the action, allowing multiple anglers to cast at once. Although not a sure thing, a timely anchor drop can produce unbelievably fast action and really maximize a catch.

In addition to a bottom-grabbing anchor, serious drift-fishermen have a sea anchor aboard. Also called a drift anchor, the device is made along the lines of a windsock, and serves to slow the drift rate in high winds. Deployed from a boat's midpoint, it helps ensure a broadside-on drift so that everyone aboard gets a chance to cast. A sea anchor also extends the time over the hot zone.

As previously noted, a trolling motor is a critical tool in successful drift-fishing. It can be used effectively when fishing slicks, mud, birds, and to assist in maintaining a straight drift in uncooperative wind and tide.

Trolling motors require maintenance. They are constantly subjected to pounding and salt spray. They require a lot of battery power and are notorious for dying at the most inopportune times. Nonetheless, they are the drifting tool you cannot do without. Without a trolling motor, you exclude yourself from a significant amount of drifting opportunities. Be it tracking slicking trout or skittish birds, trolling motors matter.

As silly as it sounds, the right landing net can make a big difference. Most boats are equipped with the wrong net. You need a three- to four-foot handled, shallow-webbed, tangle-free net. The handle length allows you to reach out and pluck a fish without having to wait until it is alongside. Shallow webbing permits quick "unloading" once the fish is in the boat. Plastic-dipped webbing reduces (but by no means eliminates) tangles that reduce fishing time. When you are on a school, the last thing you want to spend time doing is untangling fish or tackle from a landing net.

THE RIGHT BAITS

A lead-head jig with soft plastic tail is the staple artificial bait for drift-fishing. Ninety percent of the time, a jig will out-produce any other bait out of a boat.

JIGHEADS

Most anglers spend so much time worrying about choosing the right soft plastic and the right color that they overlook the most important part of a jig, the lead head. Even more commonly, anglers incorrectly choose a heavy head to increase casting distance and feel for their bait.

A heavy jighead gives you more casting distance, and the increased resistance gives better contact with the bait. The tradeoff is that the jig sinks quickly (perhaps too quickly) to the bottom, and the increased weight adversely affects lure action. Heavy jigheads have a place in deep water and current-influenced fishing around jetties or well pads. But for drifting reefs and grass flats, a 1/8- or even 1/16-ounce head is much more effective. The slow sink allows you to better cover the water column and permits the body of the soft plastic tail to drive the action of the bait. Imagine a heavy head being dragged through the water. The weight of the head kills any action of the bait outside of a paddle foot or curly tail. A light head allows the bait to "swim."

With the advent of jerkworms in saltwater, the value of a light head increased. Long, slim jerkworms produce an incredible action when paired with light jigheads. They become three-dimensional baits. These baits dart and walk not unlike the swaggering action of a walking surface plug. This 3-D action is what makes them so effective.

Always err on the side of too-light when choosing a jighead. A common complaint with light heads is that the angler loses touch with the bait. This is one of those moments you have to "use the force" and allow the bait to free-fall. The perceived loss of contact with the bait occurs from allowing it to fall naturally and simulate an injured baitfish. And this is what gets you a bite. You will be amazed how much touch you actually have even when your bait is free-falling—if you have an appropriate rod.

Save the 1/4- and 3/8-ounce heads for deep, fast water and to increase casting range when fishing under birds. A lighter head allows you to finesse fish off reefs that you never knew were there.

TAIL STYLES

Three basic styles of soft plastic should fill a drift-fisherman's tackle box: shad tails, shrimp tails and jerkworms. Although there are variations of these basic designs, these three cover the spectrum you need to be successful.

Until the mid-to-late 1990s, jerkworms were solidly within the realm of bass fishermen. Like so many imports from the freshwater world, the advent of combining a jerkworm with a light jighead revolutionized modern trout and redfish angling. I clearly remember scoffing at the first Slug-Go I saw threaded on a jighead. I resisted the trend to use jerkworms, citing better catches on shad and shrimp tails. But you can only stand to get beaten a limited number of times before you succumb to a trend. Now I cannot imagine not fishing with a jerkworm.

There are several brands to choose from, including Bass Assassin, B&L Sea Slug and Norton Sand Eel. Try several brands and go with the one that gives you the most confidence. Experiment with different worm sizes to increase the float factor. More plastic combined with less

For school-sized trout, it is hard to beat drifting mid-bay reefs.

PHOTO BY DOUG PIKE

jighead produces a more erratic action and slower sink.

The shrimp tail design is one of the oldest saltwater soft plastics, and still one of the most effective. Its straight, almost lifeless design allows it to sink quickly even without a heavy jighead and gives the angler complete control over the bait's action. It does very little without your help. This can be extremely useful when fishing a slow bite. One of my favorite slow-bite, drift-fishing baits is a plum-colored shrimp tail with a 1/16-ounce head. When nothing else works, this is my go-to combination. This bait can be darted along with slight twitches of the rod tip to simulate an inactive shrimp. Remember that when the fish you are targeting are inactive, their prey is likely inactive as well. In that situation, your goal is to present such an appealing target that the predator cannot resist the impulse to strike.

Shad tails have a lot of natural action. They can essentially be retrieved straight like a crankbait. As I once heard it said, the shad tail keeps working even when you are not working it. But just as with all soft plastics, a shad tail is going to get most of its strikes when it is free falling. Imagine the paddle tail fluttering as the bait descends to the bottom. That is appealing.

COLOR SELECTION: HOW IMPORTANT?

Color selection is a perplexing quandary for most anglers. It is no coincidence that lure manufacturers continue to produce new color combinations to lure fish and anglers alike. Anyone who has fished for long has dejectedly watched another angler catch fish after fish because he was using the latest whiz-bang color. It happens, but it is the exception rather than the rule. I have always discounted the value of color. I am still not sure if this is true or is simply a defense mechanism that allows me to not have to carry a luggage-sized tackle box.

A great way to simplify the color equation is to think in terms of light and dark. I focus on a few high-confidence colors, spending the majority of my time looking for fish instead of changing lure colors. Time spent changing baits is time spent not fishing. A general rule for drift-fishing is that clear water necessitates lighter colors, and dirty water calls for darker baits. With that said, note there are constant exceptions.

When you catch yourself maniacally changing baits and unable to catch anything, think about your "Gilligan's Island bait"—the bait you would choose if you were stranded and could have only one. Put it on and go back to fishing, not tinkering with baits.

VIEW FROM THE TOP

Topwater baits are generally associated with wade-fishing. In reality, they can be incredibly effective for drift-fishing. They will never replace a jig but can present a welcomed change from the usual reef or grass flat fare.

When drifting a grass flat, a topwater can serve as a great fish locator. One blow-up or swirl will tell you there are some fish in the area, and you can switch bait styles to capitalize on that discovery.

Anytime you see a significant amount of mullet or shad on the surface, try a topwater. Even in four to six feet of water, it is surprising how many times a trout will come up and eat on top. As exciting as catching fish on topwaters is while wading, it is twice the fun out of a boat. Think about it. When you are in a boat, you are significantly higher than when wading. You can literally look down on your bait and see the strike as it happens.

A little-used application for topwaters is under feeding gulls. Naturally, you will have to fight the gulls' attempts to grab your bait. Hooking a gull is no fun, but topwater action under birds is hot enough to justify the risk. I first started doing this in the back lakes of

Galveston's West Bay to overcome the staggering numbers of little trout in those areas. A jig would produce a strike and subsequent eight- to ten-inch trout on every cast. With a topwater, I could fend off most of the little bites and target the larger trout.

SUB-SURFACE PLUGS

Like topwaters, sub-surface plugs are not generally associated with drift-fishing, yet have a definite place in your tackle box.

The slow-sink qualities of MirrOLures and soft plastic Corkys can be deadly effective when drifting. In wintertime drifting over mid-bay reefs, a MirrOLure can outproduce a jig. With very little shad and shrimp in the bays, a trout's diet shifts to mullet and perch, which a MirrOLure mimics almost perfectly. My top color picks are CHG, 801 and 704. I prefer the 51M series even out of a boat. Although many of the greats throw 52Ms, I personally have better control of the plug's action and greater feel for where it is in the water column with the 51M series.

The B&L Corky is a limited application bait for drifting. The super-slow sink that makes it so effective when wading can be too much when drifting. Often the drift speed of the boat kills any touch with the bait, but there are exceptions.

When drifting shallow grass flats, a Corky can be extremely effective for working sand holes. Its slow sink allows you to keep the bait in the strike zone longer.

A Corky has a place in deep-water drifting as well. By bending the tail to make it dive, you can fish deeper reefs with great success. The key is to dart the Corky then come to full stop. The bent bait will corkscrew when retrieved straight. The goal is to make it dive and suspend motionless. The strike will usually occur when the bait stops.

You can adjust a Corky's sink rate by inserting small segments of finishing nails or heavy wire in the soft nose. This trick allows you to get the bait down quickly without killing its action.

The Rat-L-Trap is a successful import from freshwater. It is a semi-deep diving plug that produces a staggeringly loud BB-driven rattle. I first started using this bait while trying to coax stubborn redfish mudding in Galveston's East Bay. With a fluttered retrieve, the vibration and rattle-enhanced action worked when nothing else would. I look at the Rat-L-Trap as a specific application bait. When the fish do not want to look up, this bait has a megaphone to get their attention.

SPOONS

Although I rarely do it, there is no reason not to use a spoon when drifting. It has an incredible ability to flutter that is enhanced by a long fall in deep water. A 1/4- to 1/2-ounce gold or silver spoon is a good choice.

As when wade-fishing, try to avoid simply retrieving the bait. Use your rod tip to exaggerate the inherent crippled action of a free-falling spoon. It is also wise to use a swivel to prevent line twist.

NATURAL BAITS

There is no doubt that more trout and redfish have been caught on natural bait than by jigs, topwaters and plugs combined. Natural bait is extremely popular and very effective. For drift-fishermen, it is hard to match a live shrimp under a rattling cork.

Many bait anglers are very passive when drift-fishing. The thought is that the fish will come to the bait. To some degree this is true, but by being aggressive and working your bait, you tilt the odds in your favor.

When drifting a reef or grass flat, you should constantly work the cork. Be ready to make a lot of casts and keep a lively bait on your hook. Sedentary fishermen simply do not catch as many fish as aggressive ones. Live bait is very similar to a lure when drifting large areas of structure. You are trying to cover water to find fish. Once you find the school and anchor on them, you can become passive. Until then, keep it moving.

The main exception to the aggressive rule is when freelining croakers for trout. The croaker comes with its own "rattle;" a croaking sound draws (some say irritates to the point of violence) trout from considerable distances. It is often speculated that trout and croakers are natural enemies because of a croakers proclivity to swipe trout eggs. Regardless, they can be very effective on inactive trout. They can be difficult to use when drifting. The best method is to select a likely piece of structure (reef, rock, wreck, or grass line) and wait it out.

Even in the realm of croaker soaking, it is generally the more aggressive anglers who succeed. By looking for slicks and active bait, you can concentrate your efforts where you know there are fish.

THE NEED TO DRIFT

Drifting should not be the only strategy in your play book, but to allow it to be your weakest link is a big mistake. Everyone is capable of becoming a good drift-fisherman, and to be consistent, you have to work on your skills and develop your style. Without drift-fishing, a lot of good water goes unfished. And fishable water is a terrible thing to waste.

Chapter Five

Wading Techniques:
The Mystery and Mystique of Wade-fishing

Wade-fishing is marked by a mystique not evident in most other styles of fishing. There is a certain bond between fisherman and the elements, a sense of spirituality in being literally immersed in the environment; to those in the know, the spiritual connection will not be lost.

For the wade-fisherman, there is a connection to the environment that lends a Zen-like ability to sense the pulse of the bay, to instinctively know what the fish are doing, where they are, and what they feel. There is no guessing about the bottom structure or water temperature. You feel the tide on your legs and see the subtle movement of baitfish at your side.

There is also an element of control in wading. Without the distractions of a rocking boat or precarious elevation of a towering pier, you become a hunter stalking prey and feel like you may, for once, have the advantage.

Wading gives the angler almost infinite control over his

approach not possible by other means. He can speed up, slow down or stop instantly. He does not struggle with wind and current to achieve and maintain position. He can creep over structure or rip across a barren flat.

Wading is arguably one of the few fishing tactics employed in both salt- and freshwater that has its origin firmly grounded in briny tradition. Now growing in popularity on flooded pond and lake flats too shallow to drift and troll, wading is making its mark, exposing new areas and untouched fish to enlightened "green trout" anglers.

As in all styles of fishing, successful wading is not as simple as hopping off the boat or bank and catching fish. You have to carefully select

The author holds a topwater trophy.

your spots, know what to do when you get there, and be properly equipped to deal with changing conditions and patterns.

PICKING THE RIGHT SPOT

Even among experienced wade-fishermen, the general concept of a good wade is to pile into the water, pick a desirable depth and take off wading until your starting point is just a dot on the horizon. Although the "Hercules wade" can find fish, it often negates the importance of looking for signs, reading the water and picking the right spot.

The successful wader picks a spot with an eye to more than just a good starting point. There are times when a marathon wade across an immense grass flat or sand bar turns up schools of transient fish, but remember the idea is to locate and catch fish. Planning is called for so that more time can be spent fishing rather than blindly wading and casting.

Try to find the elements of a good pattern. Focus the meat of your wade on structure. Even if it is as subtle as a slight ledge or drop-off, pick something that will hold bait and predators. Look for baitfish and signs of active or passive feeding patterns. Once you have a solid game plan, fish it. Do not set up a good wade and rush through it. Remember that it is a lot easier to walk through a school of fish than it is to walk into one. Pick your spots for reasons that give you confidence, then fish out the pattern. Do not run away from it.

LEARN FROM OTHERS

Enough cannot be written or said to emphasize the value of learning from other anglers. You would not be reading this book if you did not believe that. From a beachfront pier in Galveston to a sand hole-covered flat in Rockport, odds are someone has fished the spot you target.

There are very few places left to pioneer. Although this can be discouraging at the outset, it can be to your advantage. Watch the spot selections of other anglers. Just as you should observe an oysterman to learn a mid-bay reef, carefully watch the spots chosen by other anglers. Do not go over or pull in on a spot where another angler is fishing. That is piracy. But make notes if a fisherman is in a likely-looking spot. This is particularly true when trying to learn a bay that is new to you. Watch where others fish, and when the spot is empty, slide in and see why that spot was chosen. Even if you catch nothing, you can feel the structure that may make the spot a first pick on a future trip.

BE A PIONEER

Just as you may walk in another's footsteps to learn a spot, try a spot that is considered foolish (not dangerous, just unlikely to produce). In fishing new areas and even new bays, I find myself more involved with looking for signs of fish rather than rushing to my next spot. If an angler does not know that a spot is a loser, he or she can fish it without prejudice. The Troutmasters tournaments of the past few years have proven this. An out-of-town angler will look at every reef or slick with unbridled optimism and address it with the same effort. Not surprisingly, tournaments have been won in areas that locals considered "dead spots."

If you see something on a shoreline or exposed reef that gives confidence for a wade, try it. Or if it is the end of your day and you are losing your focus, try a new spot regardless of its appearance. To be an expert in a bay, you need to wade every square inch of it. A formidable task, to be sure. It is hard to not go to a spot that you know has fish during the prime bite of the day, so try alternate spots during off-peak times. Granted, you will not be giving that spot a true shot at showing what its got, but you will have an opportunity to get your feet in new water and assess the potential. If you catch a few fish, you can only assume it will be much better during a primetime wade.

MID-BAY REEFS

Humps and knobs on mid-bay structure are not just for drift-fishermen. Mid-bay reefs are waded much more commonly now than in the past. Even with more anglers targeting these productive wading spots, mid-bay structures remain largely underutilized. Every hump or exposed ridge on a reef has its own personality with subtle nuances that make it unique and influence the schooling and feeding patterns of the fish on it.

The traditional "sweet spots" on any mid-bay reef are at the ends. As the reef mound tapers to a point and drops to deeper shell or surrounding mud, it creates an intercept point for trout and redfish to target baitfish. This drop-off is usually the most productive part of any reef structure, but remember that many reefs have guts and fingers that make them unique. Like fingerprints, every reef is different. Explore each one thoroughly.

In wading a hump, feel out the whole structure. A simple washout or outgrowth of shell may create the needed deviation in structure to make a sweet spot.

GRASS LINES AND POTHOLES

Subsurface sea grass, most commonly found south of the Colorado River along the Texas coast, is a significant component in some of the richest bay ecosystems on the Gulf coastline. Grass provides structure and protection for everything from the smallest baitfish to the larger game fish. It attends shallow shorelines and helps reduce turbidity and is thus associated with clean, fishable water. But just because you are on a grass-covered shoreline does not mean that you are automatically catching fish. Just

PHOTO BY PAT MURRAY

Capt. David Wright grabs an East Bay red.

like any shoreline structure, there are certain areas that simply hold more fish.

The deep side of a shoreline grass bed commonly tapers to deeper bay mud and silt. This structure change often creates a color line that serves as a natural pathway and ambush point for roaming schools of trout and redfish. By wading down this natural color line, you can address both a change in structure and water clarity. Look for subtle bends in the grass line and fingers of grass that break the continuity of the structure. Any nuance offers an ambush point for fish and anglers alike.

Potholes have been immortalized in the work of almost every coastal artist. Every angler can visualize peering into a sand hole gleaming in a meadow of thick grass, but not all potholes are like that crystalline image. Often they are distorted and blend into other holes and spots, and this is a good thing. The more irregular a hole, the better. Game fish use the structure break to ambush unsuspecting prey.

Fully exploring a pothole requires patiently fishing it with several different approaches. The temptation is to walk or jig a bait across the hole and move on to the next spot. Be patient and keep working the hole with different presentations. Try working your bait from the surrounding grass through the middle of the hole. If that does not work, try working the outside edges. If the sand hole looks good and is holding some baitfish, try every possible approach before moving on to the next spot. Sometimes it only takes one sand hole to make a trip.

COVER THE WATER

To thoroughly fish an area, you must cover the water you have selected. If you never get out of knee-deep water, you have only discovered what is— or what is—feeding at that depth. As you wade, constantly change depths until you identify a pattern. This will enable you to access different thermoclines and ranges of the structure you are targeting. The "zigzag" technique will also teach you the area. Even if you do not catch any fish on the deep range of a shoreline, you may find a transition of structure or drop-off that will produce fish in the future.

Feet are the greatest learning tool for a wade-fisherman. You have a 100-percent accurate depth finder and structure analyzer running at all times. Use it to your advantage. Even after a hard wade, on your way back to the shoreline or boat, try various wading depths. Be curious about the shoreline you are fishing. Walk every possible inch and try to create a mental map of the bottom. Just as in drift-fishing, map your wades in a notepad when you get home. Even a seemingly dead stretch of shoreline should be mapped and recorded, helping you formulate a mental picture of the bay.

A fishing guide often has a great advantage covering water on a shoreline. With three to five anglers on any given wade, each angler can employ different baits at different depths to thoroughly cover a shoreline. When one angler finds a school and effective pattern, the rest of the party can emulate and capitalize on the pattern. Even a small group can use this same tactic by spreading out and using different baits. Put one angler in shallow with a spoon or topwater to look for redfish while another goes deep with a jig to look for deep-water bites. Do not be afraid to fade in and out on the shoreline. Remember that you must find fish before you can catch them.

Even though you want to cover water, do not walk through a school of fish that you have labored so hard to find. When you catch a fish, plant your feet. The natural inclination is to keep on pace or, at least, inch forward. Unfortunately, this can quickly put you on top of or past the school you are fishing. If you catch a fish or even just get a bite or blow-up, fish it out. You may have found a viable school. One blow-up on a topwater may be all you need to know that you are on a school of fish, and a change in baits or presentation may start the ball rolling

PHOTO BY PAT MURRAY

A trout attached to a MirrOLure.

in earnest. Remember that one isolated bite is not necessarily the result of one fish but could be one fish out of an inactive school. Patience may turn that one fish into a great trip.

Sometimes drifting can be a tool of the wade-fisherman. When looking for fish on a large grass or sand flat, a drift can locate a school or at least produce a bite or two that will give you confidence for a wade. Although not recommended if other waders are around, drifting can cover open water at a faster pace than wading and allows a higher perspective to look for active baitfish, slicks or mud boils.

Do not let other anglers psyche you out of your spot. Just like another angler's footprints can teach you a new spot, do not let others' footprints discourage you from your own favorite spot. With substantial fishing pressure and a knowledgeable angling public, virgin spots do not last long on a busy weekend. Just because another angler just stomped across your favorite reef or shoreline without a bite does not mean that you cannot catch fish there. The prior angler may have caught nothing because he or she didn't know what to look for. If an area looks fundamentally good to you, fish it with confidence. How many times do you think you have waded a spot and caught fish, not knowing that a crabber or boater plowed through the area only moments before? It probably happens a lot more than any of us realize. Fish your spot, and forget about who was there before you.

USE YOUR EYES

Undeniably, wade-fishing is spot oriented. There is a limited amount of wadeable area, and historically, productive spots draw the majority of fire. It is common for anglers to ignore telling fish signs in haste to get to a particular spot. Using your eyes to read the water and look for feeding activity is not just for drift-fishermen. Use your eyes and you may not need to go to that popular spot.

SLICKS

In almost all forms of saltwater bay fishing, slicks are the most common sign that anglers target. Wade-fishing is clearly in this category. If you are fishing anything from a rich grass flat to a barren sand bar, a slick is a key sign. Just as in drift-fishing, the slick may not mean fish are feeding at that moment or may not even be caused by the species you are targeting, but it is a sign of life and activity. Watch the depth slicks are coming from and focus your efforts on that pattern. Even if they are popping from seemingly too-shallow water, let the signs drive your fishing effort.

MUD BOILS

Mud boils are a common sign for redfish on a shoreline. As redfish root through shallow mud flats they cannot help but expose themselves. Note that this cloudy sign can appear from redfish and drum when they are not feeding as well. Even a quiet wader can easily spook a group of shallow fish. That school may run to deeper cover, but the spook boil is still a good indication that there are other schools or singles in the area and is a dead-on indicator for the probable depth of other schools.

BIRDS

Birds are another common sign many waders do not fully utilize. Although birds do not actively work on shorelines as readily as in open bays, flocks of feeding gulls can be found within wading range. If you get the chance to wade under birds, it can be unbelievably fast action and give you a workout that rivals a stationary bicycle.

Inherent to "bird fishing" is fast moving schools of fish. They are actively chasing and pushing the bait as they feed. When on foot, this can translate into long, fast wades that can end with a slide to unwadable depths. The flip side is if you can stay with a flock, you can wade within casting range without blowing through the school as is common in a boat.

Just the presence of birds, active or not, can unveil a good wading spot. Cormorants and loons indicate there are baitfish on a shoreline, and pelicans are sure indicators of mullet.

Even if the birds are not actively feeding, terns and gulls pecking along the mouths of bayous and marsh outflows can be a great indicator of virtually undetectable subsurface shad and shrimp being poured onto a shoreline. On days when shoreline bait is scarce, a few birds can go a long way to put you on baitfish and, subsequently, on game fish.

BAITFISH

Reading the behavior of baitfish is an art in itself. Even the greatest anglers struggle to lock down definitive reads on what a particular action by a shad or mullet means to your wade. Like a great stock chart reader, the greats just get it right more often. But even in the murky water of interpreting baitfish movement, there are some definitive signs.

Any baitfish is positive. Never discount the value of a mullet flip or shad click, particularly when bait is scarce. But what about when the bait appears to be everywhere? What do you look for when there appears to be a splash from baitfish in every direction? This is where a look beyond the obvious can pay great dividends.

Look for lines of mullet that parallel a shoreline. On any given wade, there can be bait scattered along the length and breadth of the shoreline. Focus on areas where the mullet appear to herd into a consistent line. If you see mullet consistently jumping at a given depth, go there.

There is a big difference between a mullet casually jumping and one that is running. Generally when a mullet is running from a predator, it jumps in rapid succession and stays very close to the water. Just like an Olympic hurdler, it is trying to jump while maintaining speed.

Look for multiple mullet jumping at once or in different directions from the same spot. That is a very good indicator that they are running from something. Mullet tend to follow each other in their jumping patterns. When they fly out of the water in different directions, they are running for their lives.

Shad are a much harder read. They do not jump with any great frequency, but if you see one or more of them jump, run to that spot. Shad are the archetype of schooling fish. Their often tight packs click-

PHOTO BY PAT MURRAY

Chuck Duff puts the squeeze on an East Matagorda Trout.

ing across a shoreline or flat can be a great indicator that some predator is not only forcing them to school tightly, it is driving them to the surface. Virtually no baitfish wants to spend an inordinate amount of time on the surface where it is subject to attack from birds. So, if you see smaller baitfish such as shad or glass minnows on the surface, chances are they like the odds on the surface better than beneath it.

DIRTY WATER

Dirty water can be a positive. Trout and redfish anglers have been mercilessly brainwashed into believing that you have to have the proverbial "trout green" water to consistently catch fish. This is simply not true. Catching fish in dirty water is not only "doable," it is done often by those in the know.

Just because water appears dirty to the angler does not mean it is uninhabitable for the fish. If there is enough bait, game fish will likely be there as well. It simply takes modifying your mental need for water clarity and changing your bait selection.

Remember that bass fishermen are often subjected to long periods of dirty water due to runoff. Yet, they do not quit fishing. They simply utilize louder, flashier baits and different colors. Large, loud topwater plugs are a great tool for dirty water. They present a large silhouette and plenty of volume to attract attention.

Spoons are at their best in dirty water. Not unlike a spinnerbait in murky, flooded timber, a spoon can flash its way into the attention of trout and redfish. Their crippled flutter can be deadly, even in the muddiest conditions.

With a jig, try using a clicker or rattling cork. The extra bang and rattle of the cork can bring the fish to your bait.

Although there are no hard rules on color selection, dark baits seem to produce best in dirty water. Logically, a dark color is more easily silhouetted in dirty water and stands out against a muddy backdrop.

A crucial element for successfully wading a dirty shoreline is ignoring all the countless articles, stories and "experts" you've read and heard singing the praises of clear water and decrying the muddy. Always remember that a confident angler is a better angler. By bucking traditional wisdom, you may find yourself on a shoreline loaded with fish but not with fishermen.

ACCESSORIES

Have you ever been the object of comments entailing references to "Inspector Gadget" or "Batman and his utility belt?" Does it take you more than 20 minutes to get your gear on for a wade? Remember that you are wade-fishing not camping.

Imagine what you would want to carry if you were stalking some game animal on an African savanna. You would not want anything that would reduce your agility, stifle your stamina or impede your quickness. A long wade is no different. Your equipment should augment your performance, not encumber it.

So-called handy gadgets are the temptation of all anglers. Tackle marketers have made fortunes capitalizing on our weakness for gear that will allegedly push our fishing to the next level. It is hard to resist. Do you have an empty compartment in a tackle box? Or a storage box in your boat that has a lot of space for more gear? Of course not. Your wading gear should not reflect this pack-rat mentality.

THE BELT

There are a number of good wade-fishing belts on the market in a variety of styles. The best advice for selecting a belt is to go with what feels best. Try several, and choose the one that allows you the most maneuverability. I do suggest you go with one that provides good back support. Long wades and rough boat rides can play havoc with your back. A good belt can make a world of difference.

LURE BOXES

There are two general choices for lure box pouches. You can use a belt pouch that will hold up to two lure boxes or a double-pouch shoulder harness. Which one is best is a matter of personal preference.

I have always used a belt-mounted pouch and stuffed two boxes in it. The belt pouch is easy to access and is out of the way when slid behind you.

The shoulder harness actually provides more room for lure boxes (up to four) but is more cumbersome. It also allows you to wade without getting your lure boxes wet. Although a minor detail, it can add longevity to costly hard baits. Try on both and choose according to personal comfort.

The main problem in wading with more than two lure boxes is that you will inevitably fill them. It is an unwritten law of fishing that all empty compartments simply must be filled. You wind up carrying baits that you will never use, or you succumb to the temptation to switch baits way too often. You should carry only enough bait types to cover the water column and color spectrum. Filling your boxes should be a matter of careful selection with an eye to versatility.

PICKING YOUR BAITS

Focus on the major food groups. You want baits in a variety of sizes to cover the spectrums of depth and prey size. You must fill your boxes with baits that give you confidence. My opinion, your neighbor's opinion, and the last Troutmasters Tournament winner's opinion will all be different—and they are all irrelevant. You must select baits that give you a winning attitude.

The recommendations below provide a starting point, and nothing more. It is up to you to experiment and decide what works best for your style of fishing.

One box should be strictly solid-body baits. Have four or more topwaters in assorted styles and colors. This can change depending on the area you are fishing. (Some anglers maintain several boxes with contents customized to particular bays or water conditions—a muddy water box, clear water box, and so on. They then stuff the appropriate box in their belt pouch and get after it.) Carry two large topwaters (Super Spooks), one clear with chartreuse accents, and one solid bone. Carry a few smaller topwaters like Ghosts or Spittin' Images to balance bait sizes. Try chrome in one and 'Halloween' (black back/gold side/orange belly).

Carry several suspending and slow-sink baits, including MirrOLures (I am never without a 51MRCHG, 51MRHP and 51MR801) and Corkys (glow, hot pink and pearl with a chartreuse back). Always carry a spoon. This is your Gilligan's Island bait. I prefer a 1/4-ounce gold

Johnson Sprite. There are numerous styles and brands of spoons. Experiment with several until you find the ones that work for you, but never leave home without one. It can save a trip and make a tournament.

I subtly vary this selection depending on the focus of my trip. If I am going to the surf, I load several more MirrOLures and spoons and reduce my Corky selection to better deal with wind and associated casting problems. If I am fishing south Texas grass flats, I add more topwater size and color selections to combat clear water and spooky shallow water fish. This general formula will plug into most situations.

Filling a soft plastics box is difficult. There are so many choices of bait styles and colors, and, unfortunately, there are times when you need more than you could ever carry. With this in mind, I try to focus on the staples. I generally use 4-1/2-inch jerk worms (Bass Assassins, Sea Slugs or Sand Eels) and shrimp tails. For the past several years, I have rarely used shad tails. I feel a jerk worm does it all. I carry shrimp tails for super-slow finesse work and occasionally carry an electric blue or white/chartreuse scented shad tail for murky water.

I try to stick to light and dark colors in jerk worms. Never be without a dark red (red shad in the Assassin) and pumpkinseed with a chartreuse tail. These are go-to baits in any conditions. I carry a chartreuse for super-clear water and pure white for murky conditions. In my mind, this covers the spectrum.

I carry one color shrimp tail (plum with a white tail) for all conditions. Combined with a 1/16-ounce head, this bait can be floated over shell and grass and worked with the most subtle action. When I know there are fish in the area but I cannot get bites, this is my bait.

I pack a small selection of jigheads. Too many heads will merely rust in your box. I carry short-shanked lead heads without paint. The paint peels and just seems to distract from the color scheme of the tail. I carry 1/4-, 1/8- and 1/16-ounce heads. This will address all bay situations without burdening your box.

Recommending baits to another angler is like recommending food. Everyone has individual tastes, and we each have to choose what makes us comfortable. Constantly evaluate your bait selection. If there are baits you do not use or simply do not work for you, rotate them out. Keep an eye open for a bait to fill a hole in your repertoire, but make sure it is one that works for you and not just something you choose because it is "new." When it comes to lures, there is truly nothing new under the sun, just variations on existing themes.

THE STRINGER

There are two main choices in deciding how to retain your catch: a stringer or a Do-net. If you choose a stringer, use a thick cord style with a large float to keep your fish suspended away from bottom-dwelling scavengers. Make sure it is 15 feet long. Under 15-feet will likely put your fish too close to you if there are sharks in the area. Over 15-feet borders on ridiculous for safety and can become a tangling hazard. Stringers are effective, easy to store and a snap to clean.

The Do-net design allows you to slip your fish into a mesh bag that is suspended by a Styrofoam ring. It will keep your fish alive longer, all but eliminates the shark threat, serves as additional storage for baits, and can serve as an emergency flotation device should you step off into some unseen deep hole.

To some degree, a Do-net can be used to cull your catch in a tournament, but remember that the mesh removes critically important slime from fish. Although not immediately fatal, this abrasion exposes them to infection. Use good judgment, and do not release a fish that clearly will not survive.

The only real problem with Do-nets is that they are difficult to store on a boat. There never seems to be a compartment that will contain them.

Landing Nets

In the annals of wade-fishing, a landing net has always been taboo. Somehow it was interpreted as a sign of weakness—until the advent of big-money trout tournaments.

I must admit that I do not wade with one. I have always felt they get in my way when trying to fight and tire a big fish. On the other hand, listen closely and you will hear me cuss myself for not carrying a net when I lose a fish at my fingertips on the third grab.

There is no doubt that a net can be extremely helpful. If you are targeting flounder, a net is essential.

For now, I am not carrying a net, but if you see me on a flat with one tomorrow, do not think me weak, just practical.

Pliers and Knives

A pair of pliers tethered to a short lanyard is critical for unhooking fish and clipping line. I carry a stainless steel pair (which must be replaced annually). Although many waders go without pliers, I cannot imagine it.

I do not carry a knife. The general thinking is that a knife is useful if you ever get entangled in something. I believe that we, as fishermen, just like the idea of carrying a sharp knife around with us. Carry one if it makes you feel better, but it is one more thing to get in your way and rust.

Stingray Leggings and Reef Boots

I have encountered almost every hazardous Gulf marine life. Sharks, alligators, snakes, jellyfish, and even drunken boat drivers do not scare me like a palm-sized stingray. Even the clear water of South

Texas does not allay my fears of being hit. I am a firm believer in protective leggings. They are costly, can be cumbersome to wear and annoying to store, but they protect you against an injury you'd just as soon not experience. Ray hits are painful, dangerous and often extremely costly.

Reef boots are easier to put on and store but more costly than leggings. They provide added foot protection from sharp shell and the unlikely, but possible hit from a ray on the side of the foot. The drawback is that most do not protect more than mid-shin high, whereas leggings offer knee-to-ankle coverage.

Whichever form of protection you choose, by all means, use it. Neither of them are any good laying in a storage locker.

WADING WITH BAIT

As with many anglers, my first experiences wade-fishing involved dragging a bait bucket up and down a flat while wielding a popping cork rig for trout and redfish. It was great fun and very effective. Although just a memory now, wading with natural bait is just as effective—and fun—as ever.

Although clearly more cumbersome than the run-and-shoot tactics of lure fishing, wading with live shrimp, croakers and mud minnows can produce fish when artificials fail and add a different dimension to wade-fishing. The best thing about using bait is that you do not have to worry about what color to use.

Bait anglers can borrow a few things from their fidgety, lure-throwing counterparts. Be aggressive, and do not be afraid to try variations to your bait rig or presentation. Change cork styles if you are not getting any action and vary the depth of your bait. Just like varying retrieves with a lure, you should try your bait on every level of the water column. Do not let your bait find the fish, you find them.

Look for all the signs that lure fishermen live and die trying to track—active baitfish, slicks and anything else that looks "fishy." Do not rely on your bait to get your bites for you. Even with the seemingly unconquerable croaker, find your quarry first.

Carry various sized split shot weights for targeting different depths. Do not be afraid to take off your cork and free-line your bait. Just like using a lighter jighead to enhance a lure's action, no weight will allow your bait to swim freely. This can be a great attractant on hard-bite days.

Do not over-accessorize. With more mandatory terminal tackle involved in bait fishing, it is easy to overload yourself with leaders, weights, corks, and hooks. Pack only what you need. Pre-assemble a few rigs to address everything from free-lining to cork popping. Carry only a small assortment of replacement hooks and weights.

Your bait bucket can be a great encumbrance when wading and trying to land a fish. Try to use a short cord to tether your bucket to your belt. Oddly, if it is close, it will not get tangled as easily as on a long cord that can get wrapped around your stringer or, more dangerously, your legs. By keeping it close, you are better able to control it.

FOR THE LOVE OF WADING

Whether wading with a topwater on a pristine Mansfield grass flat or dragging a bait bucket along an industrial Galveston shoreline, there is something that separates wade-fishing from all other styles of bay fishing. There are those who would rather catch one fish wading a shoreline than a limit drifting a reef. I cannot put myself in that category. I like all of it. Still, wade-fishing is an important part of a coastal angler's game plan, and the spiritual side just makes it all the more enjoyable.

Chapter Six

Jetties:
Mystery and Diversity on the Rocks

Nowhere but the jetties can everyday anglers find the sort of epic fishing experiences usually reserved for weathered "old salts." True titans of the ocean prowl within walking distance of shore-bound fishermen. Set on a stage of granite, this is truly where the bay meets the

PHOTO BY DOUG PIKE

Outdoor writer Joe Doggett with a jetty mack.

PHOTO BY DOUG PIKE

Gulf. The jetties are literally gates between estuary and ocean. What could have more potential?

The incredible stories almost outnumber the rocks themselves. Goliath 600-pound grouper, pterodactyl-like manta rays, monster sharks, rolling tarpon, and an occasional billfish make the picture even more surreal. Incredibly, the Texas state record for tiger shark was held for years by a Port Aransas jetty angler. Nothing is out of the question on the rocks.

With unending tidal flow, miles of structure and constant exchange between bay and Gulf, jetties are the marine equivalent of a melting pot. From 72-series MirrOLures to popping corks, there are as many styles of fishing as there are species to catch.

JETTY STRUCTURE

Jetties have been created along the Texas coast and beyond to protect the mouths of ship channels and passes from the constant shift of bay siltation. For something the uninitiated might describe as a big pile of rocks, their design is surprisingly detailed. Generally, a jetty is shaped like a pyramid. The submerged base extends out beyond the visible slope of the surface. This creates a subtle drop-off that slides into

C/1

"The punisher."

Tommy Lamonte, left, unhooks a West Bay speck while Capt. Jimmy West nets one for Amber Patterson.

Edie Knighten basks in the glow of a Texas redfish.

Capt. George Knighten grabs a tournament-quality trout.

C/4

Sheepshead... a.k.a. "convict fish." This one has been captured and "put on ice."

Black drum.

A true saddle blanket.

A Texas bay shrimper.

the sand and silt at the base.

This design creates an incredible amount of very dense structure. Like a terrestrial jungle, this structure serves as habitat for all sizes and forms of marine life.

With such expansive structure, the successful angler's job starts with finding the oddities and continuity breaks that create ambush points for predators. Randomly tossing baits to or from the jetty is not enough. Although countless numbers and species of fish patrol the rocks, there are certain sweet spots that hold more fish.

Finding sweet spots in a seemingly endless pile of rocks is a matter of looking for subtleties. Any fallen rock, dip in structure, break in conformity, or sag in the channel or Gulf floor has the potential to divert tide flow and create a washout, wash over or point. Unfortunately, trial-and-error experimentation is the best method for discovering sweet spots. When walking the rocks or cruising by boat, keep your eyes keyed to the big picture of the overall layout. Look for variance, and you will find fish.

For the boat angler, a depthfinder is the perfect tool for finding subsurface structure. This underwater eye allows you to see humps that are undetectable from the surface. Set your screen to chart the bottom and constantly eye the pattern. Try looking away from the main body of the jetty rocks. Sometimes an old wreck or storm-thrown rock will be a considerable distance from the jetty. This type of oddity can become the spot of a lifetime.

OBVIOUS SIGNS

The baitfish and game fish that frequent the rocks exhibit many of the same signs as in the bay. Yet, jetty anglers tend to get so caught up in spot location that they ignore the obvious.

Although not as common as in the bay, slicks are a viable sign when jetty fishing. It is even more difficult to identify the species making the slick, but it is still a sign of activity and often an indicator of a prime ambush point where a school has fed or is feeding.

The numbers and varieties of baitfish on the jetties can be overwhelming. Use this to your advantage. Watch the bait as it cruises the rocks, look for nervous behavior and key on areas where bait concentrates. Do not pass up a mat of mullet or ball of menhaden to go to a dead spot. You may drive or walk past a school of game fish.

Birds can play a big role in locating jetty fish. As in the bay, they are constantly looking for baitfish and will capitalize on any opportunity to feed on bait being driven to the surface by game fish. Look for gulls and terns working away from the rocks. These flocks often produce Spanish mackerel, bluefish and a host of other alternate species. They can provide great fun and break up the jetty grind. Also watch for cormorants. They will commonly glide along the rocks and ambush minnows and small finfish. If you see a large concentration in one area, give it a try. They may see something that you cannot.

WASH OVERS AND WASHOUTS

Created by sags in the sea floor and the hard-hitting impact of storm surges, wash overs and washouts between the Gulf and channel side of a jetty are an easy target for boat and shore-bound anglers.

As wave action and current transfer water from different sides of the jetty, the point of exchange becomes an attraction for baitfish and game fish. Different sides of the jetty can have significantly different water clarity, salinity and even surface temperature. As water passes through the breaks, it often creates strips of off-color water that game fish use to ambush prey.

Substantial breaks in the jetty structure may indicate scattered rocks on the sea floor. If the rocks are no longer part of the above-sur-

PHOTO BY PAT MURRAY

Dr. John Murray lifts a heavy jetty red.

face structure, it is not a stretch to surmise they are on the bottom. Even if they were not pushed far from the main body of the jetty, their presence can cause washouts and rock humps near the base. These make prime targets from a boat or off the rocks.

As current moves along the base of the jetty, it is constantly moving the silt and sand that borders the rocks. With excessive current or when the force of the tide is channeled through a small gut or break in the structure, it can move and wash out large areas of the jetty floor. These holes become prime dwellings for bottom species. Always look for fingers or extensions in the jetty. The force of tide pushing around any extension will generally create a washout.

TIDE AMONG THE ROCKS

Just as in the bays, tide rules all feeding patterns. Understanding the proper timing of the bite in relation to the ebb and flow of tide is what separates two-fish and 20-fish catches. It can be literally a matter of minutes between being on the bite or being a loser. Learning the timing comes with fishing the jetties regularly. If you are on the rocks daily, you know there is a bite on the ebb of the tide on a given side of the jetty. Things like this are difficult to know if you are not out there every day, but there are some general rules that can help pattern the jetty bite.

As with most areas, some tidal movement is best. A slack tide is rarely the prime time, but remember that the best bite often takes place as the tide turns and begins to pick up flow. The general rule is that an outgoing tide is best on the channel side. The thinking is that the tide is flushing bait and game fish from the bay and channel out and around the jetties.

Incoming tide is favorable on the Gulf side because it is bringing beachfront species to the rocks and forcing clean, saline water back up the bayside channel. There are multitudes of exceptions to these rules, but they are a frame on which to weave a pattern.

During times of substantial freshwater inflow, the jetties are at their best. Regardless of the season, a big push of freshwater will force bay fish to the saline-rich flow of the jetties. A hard outgoing tide can force tremendous amounts of brackish water from the bays. This burst displaces bait and game fish as they seek higher saline conditions. As Gulf tides push back against the rocks, many of these fish will take up temporary residence along the security of the rocks. When excessive spring or fall rain clouds the bay, remember the rocks.

BAY TACTICS ON THE ROCKS

When you think of fishing the jetties, it is hard not to visualize a row of anchored boats and picket of sedentary rock anglers waiting for fate to come to them. Unfortunately for most, it never does. Yet in the bay, you rarely see anglers motionless hoping for a bite, particularly among lure fishermen. The rocks should be no different.

If the size of the jetty crowd allows it, drop your trolling motor and fish a long stretch of rocks. Parallel the structure and zigzag along, trying different depths and angles. Fish it like a bass angler might work a moss bed. If the fish will not come to you, go to them. Even the most impatient, non-jetty fisherman will enjoy this style of fishing. With bait or lures, moving around helps locate fish. When you get several bites, drop anchor and work to maximize your catch.

The same theory applies to rock-hopping anglers. Carry a light load, and move constantly, covering water just like when wade-fishing. This dramatically increases the odds for seeing fish signs and subsequently, catching fish.

Try a topwater. No joke. The rocks are not known for topwater action, but don't let that stop you. The topwater bite along a jetty can be fantastic. Topwaters are also very useful for locating fish. A pop or blow-up can tip you off to the presence of a school. Drop the trolling motor and ease along the rocks. Cast tight to the rocks and out beyond the structure. Depending on the current flow, fish can suspend a surprising distance from the rocks.

When rock-walking, throw parallel to the jetty. You can cover a lot of water this way and locate fish more quickly.

I have always preferred larger topwaters in light colors. Both the clear body with chartreuse back Heddon Super Spook and chrome with blue back Ghost are consistent producers on the rocks. The best part about topwater fishing the jetties is that you never know what is going to strike. It could be anything from a trout to a tarpon.

Spoons are great jetty tools. They can be fished at any depth, and virtually everything that swims will take a swipe at them. Carry 1/2- and 3/4-ounce spoons to contend with current variations. Try to flutter the spoon and let it free-fall along the rocks, a technique that allows you to cover more depths and often out-produces a static retrieve.

Not unlike in the bay, jigheads with soft plastic tails are probably the most popular and productive jetty lures. The same general rules apply at the jetties as in the bays, but carry heavier heads (1/4- to 1/2-ounce) to combat racing tides. Remember to carry plenty of extra jigheads. The rocks show little mercy to terminal tackle.

THE REAL THING

On the rocks, natural bait is hard to beat. From free-lined shrimp to live mullet on the bottom, natural bait often draws more attention, plus has an added advantage in the ability to lure fish away from tackle-stealing rocks. A carefully placed or drifted bait can interface the structure without becoming part of it. Although the possibilities are limitless, there are several essential rigs for fishing the rocks.

Free-lining live bait is deadly effective in most situations. With the addition of split shot weights to compensate for tide, a free-lined live shrimp, finger mullet or croaker can be drifted past the rocks and attract almost all species of game fish. With so many fish along the rocks, a live finfish helps fend off some of the pesky bait stealers that plague live shrimp.

Using a slip cork (as outlined in Chapter VII, Lures Vs. Bait) allows a jetty angler to keep the bait away from the entanglements of the rocks, yet still address the lower reaches of the water column. You can suspend a live shrimp just above the base of the jetty in 8 or 10 feet of water yet still cast it adeptly. This technique is ideal for drifting a deep-rigged bait around the washouts common to the end of jetties.

A three-way rig is equally effective for suspending a bait in deep water without adversely affecting casting ability. It allows a fast strike and is great for suspending live finfish.

CAPITALIZING ON DIVERSITY

Any angler can capitalize on the diversity of the jetties. With so many species of fish and so many ways to address them, a little flexibility greatly increases the odds of hooking something other than a rock. Fishing from a boat or rock-hopping, you can know with almost absolute certainty that there are fish in the water. If you use your eyes and move to the fish, the rocks can more than make a perfect day.

PHOTO BY DOUG PIKE

Pinfish rigged for action.

Chapter Seven

Lures v. Bait:
More contentious than the Hatfields and
McCoys, the legendary battle of
lures vs. bait rages on

THE BATTLE RAGES ON

Which is more effective, artificial lures or natural bait? It is a question for the ages. There is no "right" answer, and the argument will never go away. From friendly weekend bets to large tournaments founded on this competition, anglers commonly pick a side and are as unwavering in their beliefs and allegiance as a Chicago Cubs fan. Both lures and bait have a place in any angler's repertoire. Although many anglers would never admit it, both styles are effective and fun.

ARTIFICIAL BAITS

"Fool 'em, don't feed 'em" has become the mantra of the modern hardware purist. Actually, this proverb generally comes out when the purist has been defeated by a "bait soaker," but it is the sentiment of millions of anglers in both salt and freshwater.

Lure companies have seized the opportunity created by anglers' manic obsession with owning the right lure. The perfect lure always dangles just out of reach. Like King Arthur looking for Excalibur, we walk into tackle stores and hope to find the magic weapon that will forever change our fishing. This is why tackle shelves are longer than buffet lines and stuffed with such a diversity of lure styles, sizes and colors.

PHOTO BY PAT MURRAY

Heddon Super Spook.

Sadly, there is no Excalibur and no Lady of the Lake to find it for us. We have to stand up and select for ourselves.

Actually, if you look past the hype, glitter and glamour of advertising campaigns, picking the right baits is pretty basic. Isolate the main groupings of bait styles, select proper colors in these groups, and rig the baits correctly. You want to own a diverse group of lures to deal with every foreseeable circumstance but not so many that you are overloaded and not focusing on actual fishing.

The four major groups are topwaters, sub-surface plugs, soft plastics, and spoons. There are countless hybrids and crossovers, but these general groupings cover the bait spectrum you need to be well-equipped for the bay.

TOPWATERS

Topwaters are the apex of modern saltwater lures. Although arriving late into Texas' saltwater mainstream, topwater baits have been producing fish for decades in fresh and saltwater bays and lakes. There are few baits more exciting to fish than a topwater. It is one of the few lures that make missing a strike almost as much fun as actually catching a fish.

Topwaters can be walked, twitched and retrieved straight. Some have lips while others are as straight as a cigar. As more anglers focus on catching larger trout, the average size of topwaters has gradually increased and is still increasing with their use.

7M MirrOLure

Among the class of topwaters known as twitch baits, the MirrOLure 7M series is the quintessential offering. Its medieval design makes it an unlikely-looking finesse bait, but that is exactly the area where it excels. The 7M has very little inherent action without the subtle twitches of a light to medium-light rod tip. With its eyelet screwed into the top of its nose, a subtle twitch will give it short, wiggling dives and flash its silver or gold side-reflectors.

Patience is elemental to mastering this bait. It is not a fast bait. If you try to work it too fast or hard, it will roll and twist. It imitates a small baitfish stunned and fluttering on the surface. If you have ever watched a wounded mullet on the surface, it generally tries to suspend just under the water and will make short darts to escape any threat. The 7M possesses the unparalleled ability to imitate this action. Short, subtle strokes of the rod tip get the bait just below the surface, and by retrieving the slack, you move the bait and magnify its subtle, inherent wobble.

I have played with using a split ring to increase the bait's wobble but found that tying directly gives the best control. For slow-biting trout, this bait is a must. It can get bites, particularly from 15- to 18-inch trout, when nothing else will. I consider it a go-to bait when fickle, springtime spawn fish are not aggressively feeding and are targeting glass minnows.

Color is fairly significant with this bait. I prefer the 7MCHG, 7MCA and 7M51 patterns.

FLOATER-DIVERS

Floater-diver lures entered the Gulf mainstream fishing scene in the mid-1980s and have since disappeared with the popularity of contemporary walking-style topwaters. Nonetheless, they remain a valuable asset to serious anglers. Lipped topwaters can be one of the most effective surface baits to use when drift-fishing, wading deep structure or trying to slow-crawl a bait for cold-shocked shoreline fish.

CORDELL REDFIN

The Cordell broken-back Redfin was the first floater-diver to become popular in Texas bays. Its large size and slow wobble caught countless large trout through the late-'70s, '80s and early-'90s. To this day, my largest trout (9.2 pounds) came on a chrome/black back Cordell broken-back.

PHOTO BY DOUG PIKE

Straight-back floater-divers are the deepest divers. Their thinner girth and tighter wobble allow them to work down a foot or more, while most broken-backs seldom dig more than 6 to 8 inches.

Both broken- and straight-backs can be retrieved straight but are generally most effective when jerked just below the surface, retrieved a short distance, then allowed to slowly float back to the surface. Most strikes occur as the bait is floating to the surface or the moment it is jerked back down. Floater-divers can cover a lot of water when fished aggressively but also allow you to slow grind a cold shoreline. Broken-backs excel in this slow climate. When cold water temperatures have reduced fish metabolic rates, a broken-back presents a large silhouette that can be crawled and left dangling on the surface. It is a very tempting meal for a fish that wants a high return of food for a one-stop strike.

Even out of a slowly drifting boat, a broken-back can be slow wobbled by pointing the rod tip to the water's surface and slowly reeling. By occasionally twitching and stopping the plug, you can magnify its crippled action. When drifting shallow grass flats, a broken-back is a great fish finder.

I always place a split ring on the nose of a floater-diver to enhance its wobble. This steel ring will not contract or flatten like a loop knot under the pull of a diving bait.

Color choice in floater-divers is easy. They do not come in an overwhelming variety of choices like many other artificial baits. I prefer chrome with black back for almost all applications. Gold with black back would take a close second and red a close third. I never buy a factory-red floater-diver. They do not seem to have enough flash, and in clear water, metallic red is clearly better. I take a chrome with blue back bait and color it with a red marker, let it dry, and coat it with clear fingernail polish. This will lock in the red color and still retain the metallic undertone.

WALKING BAITS

Walking baits, so named for their back-and-forth "walking" motion, are one of the most common topwaters on the coastal fishing scene. There are anglers who throw nothing but these cigar-shaped baits, vowing they prefer to not catch anything that refuses to eat on top. That kind of dedication shows how exciting these baits can be.

Walking baits cover a lot of water and have an uncanny ability to entice a reaction from otherwise disinterested fish. They can draw strikes in shockingly deep water and are simply mesmerizing to watch stagger across the surface.

Working these baits can be difficult at first but are easily mastered with practice. The trick in walking a bait is twitching your rod tip while rhythmically and evenly retrieving. You have to coordinate the two, sort of like patting your head and rubbing your stomach. The bait does absolutely nothing that you do not make it do.

At first, lower your rod tip and begin a straight retrieve. The bait will run in a straight line with its nose slightly up. Begin to slowly shake your rod tip. The bait will begin to stagger, the forward motion teased to one side then the other. Once you have mastered the basic walk, try stopping the bait, pausing, then resuming its action. Like so many baits, the majority of strikes will come when the bait is still or has just resumed its action. Even when it is still, the slight wave action and momentum of the bait will cause its rattles to roll and make noise. This sound combined with a tempting pause in the erratic action is too much for a predator to resist.

It is impossible to stop your bait too much or for too long. Try any combination of retrieves and never stop experimenting. Once you master walking the bait, the temptation is to never stop that rhythmic action. Remember that you are imitating an erratic, injured baitfish. It is not going to swim on a steady trim.

There are several brands and styles of walking baits, and new ones come out almost daily it seems.

HEDDON SUPER SPOOK

The Heddon Super Spook is a large, lumbering bait. It has a low profile and swaggers with a resounding bang. It is a big fish bait that draws surprising reactions from little fish. It throws like a javelin and can be walked at very slow speeds to imitate all levels of baitfish activity.

I prefer three color combinations—solid bone, white belly with clear-silver sides and chartreuse back, and Halloween (black back, gold sides, orange belly). The middle hook of the Super Spook can be changed to a No. 4 or 6 to reduce tangling the otherwise mammoth hooks. Strangely, this modification seems to aid in hook-ups.

PRODUCER GHOST

The Producer Ghost sits with a high profile and has a high-pitched rattle. It walks easily and will get more blow-ups than any other topwater on the market. Unfortunately, its high profile and light weight also lead to more near-misses. This is not necessarily a bad thing. Remember that a missed strike can be a valuable sign of the presence of a sizable school.

Always attach a split ring to the tie eye. It will aid the bait's action and not flatten like a loop knot. Before purchasing a bait, check its rattle. Shake the box and make sure the Ghost's rattle is loud and uninterrupted. Some baits have sticky rattles.

Ghosts come in a wide variety of colors. I prefer chrome with chartreuse head, bone, and Halloween.

MirrOLure Top Dog and Top Dog Jr.

MirrOLure's Top Dog and Top Dog Jr. have become extremely popular. They are very durable, have an extremely compact walk, and emit a pounding rattle. These baits walk very easily and are a great starter walking bait for training. I prefer bone, Halloween, and chartreuse back and belly with gold sides.

Heddon Spittin' Image

Heddon's Spittin' Image is not an everyday bait. It is very light, hard to walk, and has a very high profile. It does not perform well in chop but can be deadly in calm water when the topwater bite is difficult. Like the 7M, it is a great finesse bait. It has small BB-style rattles and the shape of a shad or menhaden.

It can be effective on smaller trout and redfish and is a go-to when other baits are producing only blow-ups or nothing at all. As usual, a split ring is critical to increase this bait's action.

Subsurface Plugs

Sub-surface plugs are generally slow-sinking baitfish imitations. They lack the visual appeal of a topwater's action, but still produce arm-jarring strikes. They are an often-ignored component of anglers' boxes. With jerk worms and topwaters, the subsurface bait has grown neglected. To be a more consistently successful angler, you must master these baits.

Original MirrOLure

The original MirrOLure is the grandfather of all slow-sink, subsurface baits. They have been around forever and continue to catch fish.

They occupy an unusual spot in many anglers' tackle boxes. Most coastal anglers have scores of them in multiple colors but have no confidence using them. This is understandable. The 51M and 52M MirrOLures are nothing more than a rather small, colored piece of plastic with three large treble hooks crowded underneath it. It has no inherent action and appears almost antique in design—but they really work.

There really is no grand secret to properly working them. You can straight retrieve a MirrOLure to cover water, and by constantly varying speeds, convince a lot of fish to bite. The only "trick" to successfully working a MirrOLure is allowing it to free-fall. By stopping your retrieve and not taking in the slack, the bait will fall naturally toward the bottom. Even the slightest amount of pressure from the line will pull the bait to you and interrupt the fall. You have to let go of the need to be in constant contact for a second or more. What will surprise you is that you actually are in contact. The fall of the bait will maintain enough tension that even a peck at the lure will vibrate to your hand.

The lack of inherent action in a MirrOLure allows you to be the artist that paints its motion. Play with various retrieves but do not overwork it. If you jig or jerk it too hard, it will roll and twist and snag its hooks on itself or your line. Be subtle.

The 51M series is generally associated with wade-fishing while the 52M is more common with drift-fishing. I prefer using a 51M in all conditions. I have more control with it, and its slower sink allows it to suspend for longer periods.

By tying directly to the bait, you gain more control, particularly with the 51M series bait. Even the slightly thinner 52M series does not need a split ring. It has a subtle wobble that can be augmented with a ring but does not demand it.

MirrOLures have a small rattle, hence the "R" (for "Rattle") in 51MR. I have never been convinced it makes a big difference, but even a small rattle may help attract a picky eater.

To put it mildly, there are a lot of choices in MirrOLure colors. And just like fish stories, everyone has a favorite. If I could have only one color, it would be the CHG (chartreuse back and belly with gold side), but one color is not enough. I generally like bright colors and commonly use the HP (hot pink), 808 (Halloween), and 801 (orange back and belly with gold side).

CORKY

The Corky is an enigma among lures, and its creator is in the same category. When have you heard of a bait that produced the Texas state record speckled trout, consistently wins tournaments for amateurs and pros alike, yet is all but impossible to buy on the retail market? Only the B&L Corky fits this bill. At one time, shortly after the Texas state record was set, a local Houston tackle store rationed Corkys, limiting eager buyers to three baits per visit due to limited availability.

To understand this handcrafted jewel, you have to carefully examine its design. It is truly a hybrid, combining the construction of a soft plastic bait with the shape of a plug. Two posterior stabilizing fins give it a darting ability rivaled only by the antics of a jerkworm. The flexible wire that runs the length of the bait facilitates fine-tuning the action. By gently bending the tail up or down, you can exaggerate the dart. It can move in virtually any direction with the flip of a rod tip. With the ability to customize the bait's action, the possibilities are limitless.

PHOTO BY PAT MURRAY

The indomitable Corky.

In learning to properly

work a Corky, the key word to remember is "slow." Everything about this bait lends itself to a slow retrieve. It has an unmatched free-fall and ability to suspend that are only found through patience. It is not a fish finder, but it is one of the best baits to carefully work a piece of structure that you are confident has fish on it. When wading a deep piece of shell or fishing potholes, it is hard to beat a Corky. Besides, how many baits can boast a 33.13-inch, 13.65-pound Texas state record speckled trout?

I regularly carry three slow-sink Corky baits in my box—pearl with chartreuse back, glow (chartreuse) and pink back and belly with silver sides. The pink seems to produce best in clear water while pearl and glow are best in murky conditions.

RAT-L-TRAP

The Rat-L-Trap is a direct import from freshwater. Designed to create a lot of noise with many BB rattles and a super-tight wobble, this crankbait has a place in saltwater anglers' boxes. Although its deep dive makes its application more difficult while wade-fishing, it can be deadly when drifting deep reefs and jetties.

I have played with several retrieves and found a straight retrieve with an occasional stop is best. The bait will dig toward the bottom, and when stopped, falls lifeless to the bottom. When you pick it back up, it shakes and rattles while it resumes its action. It is not a subtle bait but can be very effective in murky water and on bottom-feeding redfish.

SOFT PLASTICS

The soft plastics category is immense and growing larger by the day. Once upon a time, there was the Boone Tout Tail. Experimental lure makers (Bill Norton, Paul Brown and Pete Tanner) were convinced there was more to soft plastic tails and started working on such blasphemous shapes as shad tails, eels and long shrimp tails. Now there are countless shapes, sizes and colors of plastic tails to adorn a jighead. As with most baits, I try to stick to the basics.

The most important part of a soft plastic jig is the head that

PHOTO BY PAT MURRAY

The "Gilligan's Island" tail - A plum and white tail shrimp tail.

holds and weights it. A quality tail is worthless hanging on a bad head. For most applications, use a wide-gap, short-shank leadhead without paint. The wide gap aids hookset by exposing a clear shot for the point and barb. The short shank maximizes the bait's natural action. Outside of some flounder, small finfish and very inactive game fish, everything aims for the head of the bait it is trying to eat. It is tempting to try to string a tail on a long shank hook in hope of capturing those nibble-strikers. The amount of fish you might catch with long shanks is far overshadowed by the amount of action lost in the bait. Unless you are specifically targeting short-biting flounder, shorter is better.

I do not use jigheads with paint. It quickly chips or melts and can ruin a bait box. There is probably no great harm in using them, but I am not a believer. I like plain heads.

Remember to go light and always use the lightest jighead you can. It allows more natural float, superior free-fall and gives more control of the action. Always carry a selection (1/16- to 1/2-ounce) to match any occasion.

Shrimp tails are the original saltwater worm. From the early Boone Tout Tail, the modern shrimp tail has lengthened and broadened. Now, countless brands fill tackle shop displays with colors to rival their freshwater counterparts. With the advent of the jerkworm in coastal bays, the shrimp tail, among others, has taken a backseat. Although I resisted the jerkworm trend for several years, it is impossible to argue with success. In any event, the shrimp tail still has a place in an angler's box.

Shrimp tails are very durable and stand up to repeated toothy encounters. When fishing under birds, it is hard to beat their resilience for multiple catches without having to change baits. They are also one of the best artificials to put underneath a mauler or rattling cork.

PHOTO BY PAT MURRAY

An icy trout.

I no longer carry the multitude of shrimp tails I once did. Strawberry, root beer, motor oil and pearl/chartreuse tails used to fill my boxes and carpet my boat after a fruitful trip. Now I carry a single shrimp tail, plum with white tail B&L Shrimp Tail. It is a great finesse bait that is best fished on a 1/16-ounce jighead. Out of a boat or wading, I go to it when all else fails. It is effective in all water colors but excels in murky conditions. It can be slow twitched, not unlike the crawling action of a Corky. It has very little natural action and, thus, adeptly imitates the slow-paddling fall of a shrimp seeking the protection of the bay bottom.

Shad tails, once thought to have revolutionized trout and redfish angling in the early-to-mid-1980s, have all but disappeared behind the success of the jerkworm. The draw of this bait is its Energizer Bunny-like tail that never stops moving. It produces vibration while its keel-like body keeps it straight during retrieve. Shad tails still work, but I, like so many others, just do not throw them with great regularity anymore.

I must admit in times of consistent dirty water, I have found myself drawn to scent-impregnated shad tails. The combination of a vibrating tail and pungent odor can be most effective in a slow bite or bad weather. I prefer the electric blue with a white tail and pearl with a chartreuse tail in Berkley's Power Shad. They really do stink, so remember to keep them in a resealable bag. Although they produce fish, they will also ruin a wading shirt.

The shad's action is at its best on the fall. As the bait descends, it twists and flutters. This combination can be too much for a predator to resist. Try to jig the bait along with a soft stroke of the rod tip. Too much action can make it roll and produce an unnatural action.

JERKWORMS

Jerkworms killed the shrimp tail and shad tail as surely as TV killed the radio star. I would have never guessed that the long, unruly design of a jerkworm combined with a short-shanked jighead could be so productive. It makes me wonder what design will be next. I laughed at the first Jumpin' Minnow I saw. I scoffed at the first Slug-O I saw threaded on a jighead. I cannot wait to denounce the next revolutionary innovation I encounter. I may be old school, but it does not take too many beatings for me to join the trend. I now use jerkworms with regularity.

There are a growing number of jerkworms on the market—saltwater versions, large ones, small ones, and a host of other configurations. In my thinking, it is hard to beat the Bass Assassin. Its very soft, supple construction and whip tail produce incredible action. When combined with an appropriately light jighead, it is incredible at any depth. It goes beyond the up and down motion of a jigged shrimp or shad tail. It exhibits a side-to-side action that borders on outrageous, and trout, redfish and every other predator cannot resist it.

The best action is created by subtle rod motions. Let it free-fall, then give it a slight twitch. It will come alive with a dart to the side. It can even be walked like a sub-surface topwater. The possibilities with this bait are unlimited.

The one downside to a jerkworm is an inherent tendency to spin. They can ruin a spool of line if rigged incorrectly. I am a firm believer in rigging all soft plastics with an obsessive compulsion to see that they run straight. Any imperfection in rigging is magnified with every rod motion. If you use a spinning reel, you almost have to use a swivel to prevent a bird nest from forming on your spool.

With a conventional bait-casting rig, a properly rigged jerkworm does not need a swivel. You still get some twisting, but occasionally trailing the line behind a moving boat will straighten it right out. Eventually, the twisting makes it necessary to change line, and there is no such thing as changing line too often.

Since jerkworms constitute the majority of my soft plastics, I carry a lot of colors. My go-to is the dark red (red shad) Bass Assassin. I like it in all water color situations. I also regularly use pumpkinseed with chartreuse tail, pearl, glow with chartreuse tail, and limetreuse (an outrageous combination of lime, green and chartreuse). I seem to get hooked on certain color combinations for short periods but always return to the basics when it really counts.

SPOONS

Spoons will never go away. They are a "Gilligan's Island bait," a survival tool. Everything will strike a spoon. From speckled trout to roosterfish, the crippled flutter of a well-placed spoon exhibits everything a predator is looking for in an easy meal. It has flash, vibration and the look of a baitfish fighting to stay buoyant. Although the spoon is clearly out of vogue, I cannot imagine setting off on a wade or even a drift without 1/4- and 1/2-ounce gold and silver spoons.

The spoon is the ultimate all-terrain lure. It can be ripped across the surface of a grass flat or slow rolled along the edge of a jetty. The weedless 1/4-ounce gold Johnson spoon is a must for redfish along South Texas grass flats, just as the 1/4-ounce gold Johnson Sprite is a must on the redfish-laden mud and shell shorelines of the upper Texas and southern Louisiana coasts.

Spoons are one of the few baits that I rig with a split ring and swivel. To properly fish a spoon, you must retrieve it with frequent, sweeping motions of the rod tip to lift the spoon and let it flutter back down. Although a straight retrieve will produce, this erratic action maximizes the spoon's action.

Capt. David Wright showed me the incredibly persuasive action of a fluttered spoon. He does not use any intermediary attachment to the spoon. Without a split ring or swivel, he ties directly to the rough-cut hole at the head of the spoon. With this arrangement, he jigs the bait to twist up and then flutter back, thus aiding in unrolling the twisting line. I could never capture that action without adding a swivel. I recommend at least starting out with a swivel and experiment later with removing it.

There are a wide variety of spoons on the market. I have always used Johnson spoons because they are the Band-Aid™ brand name of the spoon world. As previously mentioned, my stubbornness has made me recant many missed opportunities at pioneering new bait styles. Use what makes you confident and know that the Johnson spoons are likely not going away anytime soon.

MEET ME BY THE POOL

Years ago, a local Coastal Conservation Association chapter asked me to give a poolside seminar on how to work baits. Intrigued by the idea, I packed up my favorite baits and went to work the various baits. It forever changed my outlook on working lures.

If you lack confidence in your ability to fish with artificial lures or feel that you never have contact with your baits, go to a pool. It does not have to be a particularly large pool, but it does help. Try every bait with every conceivable type of action.

Note the slow, manatee-like action of a Corky. Flutter a spoon and observe the almost absurd amount of vibration and flash it produces. The most revealing to me was working a clicker cork with a soft plastic tail under it. It is incredible how much action a cork produces with a shrimp tail—or any tail, for that matter. Slack created with every click of the cork makes the bait rise and freely settle back down. You can gauge the sink rate of everything from a MirrOLure to a shad tail. It is also the perfect arena to convince yourself of the added action that comes with using light jigheads. Try a jerkworm with a 1/16-ounce head, then a 1/4-ounce. You will be astounded.

If you are really dedicated, take the hooks off your baits and have a friend work them as you submerge with a diver's mask. Watch the baits as they move through the water column and examine the look of a bait while it free-falls. You will never look at your lures the same way again.

ADDING A PERSONAL TOUCH

With a variety of tail dips and at-home lure coloring kits available, it is worth playing with bait customizing. Be careful to not go overboard. I clearly remember a period when trout in the Bolivar pocket would eat nothing but a red topwater. That brief period caused me to color everything but my wife in a shade of red. The pattern shifted, and I had an overload of red baits. Experiment with judicious discretion.

Try adding a white tail-dip to some of your soft plastics. Add another dark eye dot to the tail of a topwater or a colorful skirt to the back hook of a broken-back plug. You can easily add shades and stripes of color to almost all hard plugs and seal it with clear fingernail polish. It is a fun way to add a personal and productive touch to any bait.

SMELLY SPRAYS AND DIPS

What could make your lure better imitate an injured baitfish or crustacean? The answer is simple: smell. For years, bass anglers have used sprays and dips to enhance the appeal of their artificial offerings. These glitter-filled, synthetic stinks do make a difference; ask any bass pro. Try that same question on a local saltwater guide or tournament pro. You may be surprised that most do not use any smell additive on their lures. I am not sure why. I must admit that I have experimented successfully with them but have never fully implemented spray attractants into my fishing rituals.

I have seen them make a notable difference in deep-water fishing and in hot water conditions when fish seemed reluctant to strike anything. Just like the scent-impregnated soft plastics, spray and dip attractants have a place in every angler's arsenal.

NATURAL BAITS

This is where it all began. I can imagine early hook-and-line fishermen using natural baits to gradually crawl up the food chain. You use a shrimp to catch a piggy perch, that allows you to catch a speckled trout. It is a logical progression. Just as thousands of years ago, natural-

PHOTO BY DOUG PIKE

A Texas live bait quartet.

bait is an incredibly productive way to fish.

There is no doubt that there are times when natural bait will out-produce artificial lures. I have lived through plenty of those experiences (not always on the winning side). Just as in lure fishing, there is an art to natural bait fishing. And just as a lure fisherman may be called a purist, there are natural-bait purists as well.

My most common advice to bait fishermen is to be aggressive. Do not place all your eggs in your bait bucket and depend on its inherent attractant qualities to bring fish to you. Do not become passive just because you are using the real thing. Be aggressive; use every fish sign you can to better your odds. Being pro-active and mobile is one of the main reasons lure fishermen ever out-produce live bait anglers.

Just because you have the real deal does not mean you can hang every conceivable snap, bead and weight on a terminal rig and expect to catch fish. Fish have eyes to avoid those types of traps. Try to fish with the least possible amount of terminal gear to reduce the signs of man on your bait and to allow it to swim freely.

Chumming is not just for offshore fishing. Try using some portion of live or dead bait for chum. Not that you should let a pint of precious and expensive live shrimp disperse into the bay, but try cast-netting shad or minnows to release when you are anchored on a spot. Try smashing the heads of a handful of dead shrimp to create an ooze of pungent shrimp juice. Predator fish use their olfactory sense to follow the chum line to its source—you and your baited hook.

Identify positive fish signs before chumming. There's no point fishing where there are no signs—and therefore no fish—and there is no point chumming under like circumstances.

AERATORS

You may have noted herein repeated use of the term "natural bait" as opposed to "live bait." Natural baits need not be live. Cut bait is not live, but it is natural. A good aerator helps ensure that expensive live bait does not prematurely become natural dead bait.

Buy the best aerator you can afford. If you are a pier stalker or fish the bay from a boat, a good aerator is crucial equipment. Considering what is typically spent to finance a day of fishing (fuel and other boat related costs, food, bait, etc.), it makes no sense to trust the success of the trip to a $5, single D-cell-powered bubbler. It is like going into space with a cheap air tank. Your bait will die sooner than later, leaving you with a bucket full of expensive chum and, most likely, no fish. Don't scrimp when purchasing an aerator.

The increased popularity of live croaker for speckled trout has led to a plethora of innovations in water additives for maintaining baitfish. Many of these additives are available at aquarium and tackle stores.

Make sure your bait container is insulated. Even a well-oxygenated plastic bucket full of hot water is a death trap for live baitfish. An insulated cooler makes a great baitwell. If it is really hot, add ice enclosed in a plastic bag (the bag prevents chlorine, in water used to make the ice, from contaminating the livewell). The decrease in water temperature will reduce the bait's metabolism and extend its life. Be careful not to get the water too cold. You can shock the bait when you eventually try to fish with it in the warm bay water.

CAST NETS

Always carry a cast net. Any serious bait fisherman needs a cast net to explore different baits (many of which are not sold in retail bait shops) and to ensure having bait for a trip. If the bait store does not have any shrimp, mud minnows, croakers, or any of the other traditional live baits, a cast net and marsh canal can create all the bait you will need.

Cast-netting can become a hobby in itself. It is a great learning experience to probe the depths of a boat-ramp dock or tide pool with a net. You learn about the marsh ecosystem and produce buckets of viable live bait at the same time.

BAIT RIGS

There are as many conceivable bait rigs as there are baits to use on them. There are several basic rigs that apply to almost all styles of fishing.

STANDARD POPPING CORK RIG

The standard popping cork rig is the heart of coastal trout and redfish angling. The design is time-proven and simple. Attach a popping—or better yet—rattling cork above an adjustable length of line and a small black swivel with 18 inches of shock leader, terminated with a No. 6 or 8 treble hook. This rig has probably caught more trout than any other.

This rig casts well and offers the added attraction of sound to entice trout and reds. By adding split shot weights, you can inhibit the movement of larger shrimp to keep them in the lower levels of the water column. I have experimented with adding two or more red beads on the leader line to add color and a clicking noise when the rig is jerked. This borders on the too-much-gear principle I so adamantly preach, but it is worth trying during tough times.

FISH-FINDER RIG

The fish-finder rig is a universal bottom rig that has been around for countless years. String an egg weight on your main line, then tie on a small, black barrel swivel. Add an 18-inch shock leader to the other end of the swivel and terminate with a hook suitable to the application. This rig allows your bait, live or dead, to drift in the current and presumably "find" fish.

The rig can be dragged across open bay bottom and is a deadly effective flounder finder rig for targeting migrating fall fish. This rig can be adapted to fish dead crab for redfish at jetties or soaking croakers for large trout on bay reefs. Like the popping cork rig, it is a rig for all seasons, baits and fish.

FREE-LINE RIG

The free-line rig epitomizes the "less is more" principle. It is simplicity itself, just a hook on the end of your line.

When fishing heavy cover, you may need to attach a short length of 15- to 25-pound-test shock leader to your main line. I know, I know,

I said I don't use leaders. Nonetheless, I am not so hardheaded as to willingly handicap myself through pedantic adherence to personal prejudice. If you go leaderless, remember to constantly check the line directly above the hook. Abrasion happens fast if you are catching toothy fish or working shell or barnacle-encrusted petroleum platforms.

If strong current drives your bait to the surface, try pinching on a split shot or two at least 18 inches above the bait. Use only enough weight to keep the bait down.

THREE-WAY FLOAT RIG

The three-way float rig facilitates fishing deeper with a cork rig without creating casting problems. Attach your main line to one eye of a three-way swivel. To the second eye, attach a length of leader material with a float on one end. To the third eye, attach another length of leader material to which you have attached a hook. By splitting the total length of the rig with the three-way swivel, you also increase your ability to set the hook on a fish. If you have 3 feet of line on the float side and 3 feet on the bait side, you can fish 6 feet under the surface and still control your cast and ensure a slack-free hookset.

This rig is very effective for suspending a live finfish along the deep edges of a bay reef or Gulf jetty.

SLIP-CORK RIG

A slip-cork rig allows you to fish great depths without having an impossible length of rig material to cast. Thread the main line through a float, then tie on a swivel. Attach an 18-inch leader with hook to the other swivel eye. The float slides freely up and down the mainline. To set the depth, tie a section of rubber band at the appropriate point on the line above the float. This simple rig is exceptional around deep jetties and spillway discharges. It is easy to cast but can be troublesome when setting the hook.

THE PLAYERS

From the obscure sea lice to the common finger mullet, there are innumerable possibilities in natural baits. Each has its application. The players in this game vary in size, stamina and accessibility, but all can be used as a viable form of bait.

SHRIMP

Shrimp are the bread of the sea. Everything likes to eat shrimp, live and dead. If there is such a thing as reincarnation, I am sure that very bad people come back as shrimp. Imagine being chased by everything from shrimp boats to seagulls. Live or dead, it is hard to beat a shrimp. They are available at most bait shops and survive reasonably well in an aerated cooler.

There are two places to hook a shrimp without killing it: the last body segment before the tail and under the horn or collar of its carapace (be careful to avoid the dark spot that marks the brain).

Fresh dead shrimp can be a great bait for almost any bottom feeder. By peeling the shell off the tail meat, you release additional smell and enable easier penetration of a hidden hook.

MUD MINNOWS

Mud minnows are available at most bait shops during the peak of the fall flounder migration, but they are equally accessible in many marsh pools and tidal stands. They are incredibly durable and can live in surprisingly warm, dirty and under-oxygenated water. Their marsh origins have prepared these critters for hard living. This can be very advantageous for transporting and when rigged through the lips on a fish-finder rig that is not finding fish, they just seem to live forever.

Although mud minnows are commonly associated with flounder fishing, they can produce redfish and trout as well.

MULLET

Mullet on a fish-finder or free-line rig is deadly for trout and redfish. Drifted down a jetty or sight-cast into a grass-flat pothole, a 3- to 5-inch finger mullet can be too much for a predator to resist. They are an equally deadly flounder bait. Some dedicated flounder groupies prefer finger mullet over mud minnows.

When rigged through the lips, mullet can remain lively for a long time. When they die, they make great dead bait for redfish and most other bottom feeders.

SHAD

Shad are very easy to catch along piers, boat docks and subdivision canals during the summer. They make great trout and redfish bait but are almost impossible to keep alive. With an oxygenation system, round aerator tank and ice bag, you can keep them alive for a short period, but do not bet the success of your trip on them. They are an effective dead bait and serve as a flashy chum for bay and nearshore fishing.

GLASS MINNOWS

Glass minnows, so named for their transparent bodies, are common sights under night lights. They can be caught with a small dip net and are very effective when fishing under lights. The best rig is a small No. 10 treble hook through the minnow's lips or just under its nearly invisible dorsal fin. I have never seen them in any bait shop, so go prepared with a thin-mesh dip net.

PIGGY PERCH

Piggy perch, often confused with the more common pinfish, are marked with a spiral of colors and emit a telltale grunt. Although pinfish are an effective bait, the piggy has greater appeal to finicky summertime trout. Not unlike the croaker, the piggy is best rigged with a Kahle hook behind the dorsal or anal fin on a free-line or fish-finder rig.

CROAKER

Croakers as bait has come under much scrutiny from the late 1990s to the present. Because of their unparalleled effectiveness, some have called for them to be outlawed for bait or declared a game fish. At this point, both propositions seem unlikely.

The debate over croakers serves to illustrate just how effective they are for taking trout. They are particularly effective on big fish and work under a variety of conditions. Good as croakers are, nothing is 100-percent effective. Granted, croakers often produce when nothing else will, but fishing is always fishing, and no bait is the A-bomb. Even gill nets are not 100-percent effective.

Chapter Eight

Night Fishing:
The many shades of night

You are immersed in darkness. Wading in water barely above your knees, you plod through the thin, bay-bottom vegetation. Your senses are heightened. The vague moon and starlight reveal a glimmering, oily sheen at the edge of your vision. The smell of a slick is unmistakable. You hear the mindless slap of mullet jumping in all directions. Even the buzz of a mosquito orbiting your head is amplified.

Your bait quickly disappears as you cast into the darkness. The rattle of the walking topwater clicks a tempo. Its rhythm mesmerizes you. You hear a pop in the darkness. Your rod tip drops as you stop the bait and wonder if it was a blow-up. You resume the retrieve, and your line tightens in concert with the loud crash of a trout exploding on your plug. You are on. It is dark. There is nothing better than catching a trout on top at night.

There is another much less appealing yet much more common experience when night-wading. Imagine standing in your mother's clos-

PHOTO BY PAT MURRAY

A setting sun does not mean the end of a day of fishing.

et in the dark... alone. Imagine your mom's closet because there is absolutely nothing for you to do, and you probably feel a little uncomfortable as well. That is night wading when you are not "getting 'em."

You never notice how much the surroundings of marsh grass, shorebirds and the whole coastal setting fills the empty spaces of a wade. At night, there is nothing. It is not for the inexperienced or faint of heart.

If nighttime angling is your calling, there are a lot of options for success. From light-hopping a beachfront pier to wading a back-bay shoreline, night can be the best time of the day.

NIGHT WADING

Night wading can be the best of times or the worst. If you are "on," it is an unbelievable thrill. If not, you have never felt more bored. If you decide to try a night wade, there are a few tricks that can make it a lot easier, safer and more successful.

For your first ventures, make sure you select a spot that you are very familiar wading. Try to enter from shore rather than by boat. Running a boat at night can be very difficult and dangerous. You do not need that added distraction on your first few wades.

Pick an area that has familiar bottom structure. Remember that it will be very dark. You do not want to struggle to remember where structure elements—or drop-offs—are located; you must know.

Do not take much equipment on a night wade. Try to streamline your gear down to a few select baits and essential attachments on your wading belt.

Wear a life jacket. It is advisable to wear a life jacket even during daytime wades. At night, it is critical. With so many slim, inflatable designs now available, the bulky, cumbersome life jackets of yore are no longer an excuse to go without one.

Just because it is night, do not forget to look and listen for fish signs. If there is enough moon or starlight, look for slicks and moving bait. Listen for mullet and other baitfish activity. Active bait means as much or more at night than it does in daylight.

Play the tide. Although I have no hard rules for tide direction when night wading, I firmly believe in wading a flooded shoreline. With a large high tide, there will be a greater number of predators pulling into shallow water to capitalize on the baitfish bounty.

Spring high tides can produce some of the best night wades. The lure of spawning or of seeking a post-spawn meal can put tremendous numbers of big trout on back-bay shorelines at night.

The moon and stars are elemental components of a successful night wade. At first brush, my inclination was always to wade the brightest full moon. It clearly makes the details of your wade easier to distinguish. At times, it is shocking how well you can see once your eyes are completely acclimated. However, a big moon is not always necessary or desirable. The optimum is a clear sky. Some of my best night wades have been with moderate moonlight and bright stars. This more subtle illumination gives adequate light to fish by while maintaining a significant edge and sense of security for predators.

Like so many anglers, my first nocturnal wades were a reaction to hot, crowded summer days when the day bite seemed stifled by moon-bright nights. There is logic to this pattern. Heat and crowds push fish off shorelines, and the cooler water of night provides longer feeding periods.

Before you wade an area at night, scout it carefully during daylight. Check the water clarity and look for active baitfish. If you do not see or hear much at night, you will have confidence from seeing some legitimate fish signs earlier that evening. Equally, if you do not see signs of baitfish in daylight, you may want to pick another spot.

Large dark baits produce best at night. The theory is that, although seemingly opposite, a dark bait is more apparent to fish at night when seen in silhouette against the bright surface. Thus, black baits present the largest profile and silhouette. Bass anglers have long targeted large bass at night with black topwaters, buzzbaits and even worms. Trout are no different.

A night wade box should have several black topwater plugs with loud rattles. If your favorite brand of surface plug does not come in black, simply spray paint it. MirrOLure makes a black Top Dog that is extremely productive.

It is hard to find a more consistent nighttime topwater than a spray-painted black Ghost. I believe the Ghost's higher-pitched rattle and high-profile surface presentation makes it very attractive at night.

Make sure your hooks are sharp. At night, you need all the hook-setting advantages you can get.

When walking a topwater at night, stop the bait frequently and for extended periods. You will be surprised how many fish you hook while the bait is dead still.

Although it is tempting to always throw a topwater, subsurface baits are incredibly effective and are an important part of a complete night-wade box.

Daniel Murray (author's son) shows the spoils of a successful night fishing trip.

In slow-sink baits, try a dark 51MR MirrOLure. L&S Tackle makes a black version as well as several other prime night colors, including the 51MR808 (black back, gold sides, orange belly) and 51MRCA (candy apple red). Unlike when day fishing, I almost exclusively use a straight retrieve with subsurface plugs at night. I believe it gives the fish an easy target to lock on and still aptly imitates a fleeing mullet.

Although completely unorthodox, try painting one side of a 1/2-

ounce silver spoon black . The spoon will still have one chrome side to reflect what little moon and starlight penetrates from the surface, and a black side to fill in the silhouette. Larger spoons produce more vibration and up the odds of a predator picking up its presence. Like the buzzbaits and large-bladed spinnerbaits of bass fishermen, the increased flutter and vibration attracts more attention to your bait.

No box, night or day, is complete without a small selection of dark red or plum soft plastic tails and jigheads. As always, go with as light a jighead as you can possibly throw. You want maximum float and suspension.

Pack several jerkworms and even shad tails. Both baits produce a lot of motion and vibration. Remember that every sensation is magnified at night for anglers and fish alike.

I strongly recommend a small, wade-fisherman's dip net. At night, it is a Herculean feat to land a frisky trout with a MirrOLure or topwater pinned on the outside of its mouth. It is a lot easier to subdue a fish with a net and untangle the mess after it is on a stringer than to grab a fish—or handful of hooks—in limited light.

The most important tool for night wading is a small but powerful penlight with a lanyard. You will need it to tie knots, land and unhook fish, signal approaching boats of your presence, and to get a general feeling for where you are. Make sure you buy one that is ultralight and has a gasket seal for its battery compartment.

Very few penlights last long on the bay. Saltwater tends to harshly impact any battery-operated item, but try to get one that will last at least a full season. Make sure it is attached to you so when you drop it (and you will), it is not shining at you from the bay bottom. Strange as it sounds, select one that will fit comfortably in your mouth. When you need the use of both hands to tie on a bait or land a fish, your mouth serves as a much-needed third hand.

Among the most durable and lightweight lights are the new white LED models. Some are as small as a roll of breath mints. Despite their diminutive proportions, the brilliant white light is more than ample for most chores, and on a clear night, can be seen by approaching boats from distances of a mile or more. Most are waterproof to at least 50 feet and float when powered by lightweight lithium cells. Battery life is up to 100 times that of incandescent lights, and the "bulbs" last virtually forever. The white LED light has much less effect on your night vision, too.

There are a number of LED light manufacturers. The C. Crane Co. sells several models ranging from single AA cell units to multiple-LED models that run on three C cells. All are waterproof and virtually indestructible.

Another good source is the LED Light Co., which makes both lightweight plastic models in a variety of configurations, as well as a very small machined aluminum model.

Another option to consider in either LED or incandescent lights is a headlamp. These come in several configurations, from models that clip on the brim of a hat to headband styles.

PIERS

Beachfront and bay piers offer nighttime fishing fraught with much less peril than a night wade. They are dry, safe and offer an easy opportunity for night fishing under lights. Most public coastal piers charge a modest fee for an evening of access, and when the sun goes down and the lights come up, the trout fishing is simply fantastic. Although often smaller fish, summertime light fishing can be fast and easy.

Piers come in all shapes and sizes, but regardless of layout, never ignore any available light. Fish every unoccupied light until you find a school of fish. Just as in wade-fishing or drifting, stop when you locate a school.

When light fishing is on, it is hard to find a bait that doesn't work; literally anything will work. The general rule in light fishing is the exact opposite of night wade-fishing. Under lights, a small, clear lure is best. It meets the old fly fishing dictum to "match the hatch."

Pier lights generate heat and, of course, light. This in turn activates plankton on which glass minnows, shad and shrimp forage. When small baitfish congregate, predators soon follow. Because so many of the baitfish drawn to lights are small, trout and other game fish are better attracted by small lures. I firmly believe that the smaller silhouette of these smaller baits also appear much less artificial than a large bait under the scrutiny of bright lights.

PHOTO BY DOUG PIKE

The author with a night light trout.

When fish are feeding with complete abandon, a cigarette butt would probably draw a strike. A smaller target presents less opportunity for a shining hook or sagging split ring to give away an impostor. Try a 2- to 3-inch clear glitter tube lure on a 1/16-ounce jighead or a glow with chartreuse tail Bass Assassin on an ultralight jighead. There are a host of small crappie lures that work great on finicky trout under lights.

Going small applies to more than lures. It is also true for line. I prefer a light line and no leader when fishing under lights. Although you have to be very mindful of teeth and gill plates, 8- to 10-pound-test elicits more bites than heavier line and leaders. Even if you loose a few fish to abrasion and pier pilings, the additional bites make up for it.

It is hard to beat a free-lined shrimp, shad or glass minnow under lights. This is what the fish are eating, and close scrutiny under bright light does not matter when your bait is the real thing. By cast- or dip-netting small shad and glass minnows or going the easy route and buying a quart of live shrimp, you greatly increase the odds of catching fish if you happen to hit a tough-bite.

Even with live bait, I still recommend no leader, but I would definitely ramp up to 12-pound-test line. Attach a No. 8 or 10 bronze treble hook and let the bait swim freely under the light. I believe a bronze hook is imperative in this type of fishing. The dark hook does not reflect light and will not be easily detected. Further, when a fish does break off or is released after swallowing the hook, bronze will decompose rapidly and leave the fish alive and uninjured.

If necessary, add a small split shot at least 12 inches above the bait. This will maintain the bait's natural look while getting it lower in the water column.

Be aggressive with your bait. Move it around within the lighted area. Let it swim for a few minutes, and if nothing happens, pick it up and ease it to the other side of the light. Try to focus on the edges of the light and do not be afraid to put your bait in the darkness. Often a school and particularly larger fish will be on the edges, utilizing the light-dark transition zone as an ambush point.

Change baits if your shrimp or minnow begins to die. Do not waste your time with dead bait if you are trying for trout. Not that trout will not eat dead bait, but you need to present the best bait you have until you figure out the pattern.

On a pier, hooking and fighting a keeper fish is only half the battle. Getting the fish from the water up to the boards is the other half. Particularly on stilt-legged beach piers, the journey up can lead to a lot of accidental releases. The easiest way to alleviate this problem is with a simple hoop-style crab net. Although specialized "pier landing nets" are available, they are considerably more expensive. Besides, a crab net works just as well.

Depending on the size fish you are targeting, you can purchase an appropriate hoop-style crab net, attach a long piece of heavy cord, and lower your improvised "landing net" down to the fish. You will need help to get the net to the water and back as you lead the fish into the net, but company on a public pier is rarely a problem. When the rim of the net is just under the water's surface, lead the fish into the rim, then pull the net up to the rail. If the fish is too small, you can unhook it and gently lower it back to the water, thus avoiding a fish-killing "rail-dive."

One of the best things about a pier is that it offers an opportunity for an early morning fishing session before a morning wade. When the surf is green and you are anxiously clawing to get to the second or third bar, go a few hours early and get in some action before the morning bell rings. You may make your trip before it even begins.

MAKING YOUR OWN LIGHT

The evolution of fishing lights has been dramatic. From generators and 1000-watt train lights to gunwale-mounted green lights, there are a lot of options for do-it-yourself night fishermen.

My first dealings fishing with train lights (a box of four 250-watt-bulbs on an elevated stand) and a generator was fishing a warm-water power plant discharge in winter. The hum and smoke of the generator and scorching beam from the train lights created an industrial and mildly unpleasant feel, but the fishing was so fine I scarcely noticed. Trout and redfish were schooled in the warm discharge from the local power plant. The lights only served to further concentrate the schools and add extra incentive for them to feed.

The positive in train lights or 1000-watt bulbs is their reach into the water from shore. If you do not have boat or pier access to a lighted spot, they can be a great alternative for night fishing. Although they can be setup anywhere your generator and light cord allow you to go, the best areas are generally around some structure, pass or discharge where fish naturally congregate. You can go to a somewhat captive structure-oriented audience, and the light creates the secondary structure necessary to draw more baitfish and, subsequently, game fish.

Green lights are the newest wave in fishing lights. Depending on the type, they run on battery or 110-volt power. They cast a subtle yet penetrating light that attracts and holds fish as well as—if not better than—cumbersome 1000-watters. Some can be submerged to shine from the bottom like a green pool light, while others are affixed above the water to cast light on and beneath the surface. They do not use a lot of energy nor produce noise and searing heat. The only drawback is they lack the flexibility and reach that a generator and train light provides.

I believe green lights likely do attract more fish when affixed to a boat or pier to shine across the water. Train lights find their niche when used to project out over a large area and light deep structure. Submerged lights provide great light penetration but make catching a lot harder. With the light behind them as opposed to shining down on the water, fish have the advantage and can see the slightest imperfection in any offering.

There are many different shades of night fishing. From the excitement of night wading to the ease of light fishing, nighttime can provide a great alternative to the grind, heat and crowds that often fill the day. Plus, it lends a whole new perspective to the coastal angling experience.

Chapter Nine

The "A Team"
Trout, Redfish and Flounder Basics

Speckled trout, redfish and flounder are the focus species for the majority of western Gulf coast inshore anglers. Dubbed the "Texas Big Three", these are the players that books are written about, tournaments are created for, and that become lifetime pursuits for many anglers.

Most anglers will accept any of the Big Three gladly as a stringer fish or a credited release for the day's tally, but it is rare to see someone who excels at catching all three. Generally, the diverse life cycles and patterns exclude proficiency in catching the toothsome triumvirate with regularity, and any day that brings a Texas bay slam is an achievement.

SPECKLED TROUT

Cynoscion nebulosis, speckled trout, spotted sea trout, speck, and a host of regional sobriquets apply to this popular coastal species. Most commonly caught in the Gulf and South Atlantic region, they are found far into the bays and estuaries of Mid-Atlantic states.

They are ferocious predators and feed on whatever forage species are most available and abundant. Shrimp, shad, mullet, glass minnows, croaker, pinfish, piggy perch, sand trout, juvenile squid, and virtually anything else that appears on a hungry trout's radar screen is fair game, including its own young.

PHOTO BY PAT MURRAY

Duane Grossman displays a thick springtime trout.

Due to their fine, white meat, speckled trout were actively harvested by commercial anglers until net bans swept across the Gulf States in the 1980s and '90s. It is arguable that there would not be a semblance of the trout populations currently enjoyed in the Gulf if not for the successful battles of Coastal Conservation Association (then the Gulf Coast Conservation Association) and its army of volunteers. With virtually no commercial fishing for speckled trout among the Gulf States, the recovery and restoration of the population has been remarkable.

Lacking the hearty constitution of redfish, speckled trout can easily fall prey to harsh winter freezes even in the relentless heat of South Texas. With their proclivity to hang on shallow flats, quick and unyielding arctic fronts can decimate a speckled trout population in a short stretch of icy days. With the urbanization of many coastal marshes and estuaries, it is difficult for post-freeze populations to rebuild stocks quickly. However, recent strides in hatchery-reared speckled trout raise the prospect of a manmade recovery system.

With more "manmade" juvenile speckled trout released in Texas bays each year, the possibility exists for a decimated, post-freeze population to be supplementally restored with hatchery fish. Although the young transplants would not be of great size immediately, they could represent a spawning class that might not otherwise exist. With shrinking estuaries and swelling angler numbers, it presents an alluring prospect for the future.

Although a weakfish in both constitution and namesake, speckled trout are surprisingly adaptable. They can tolerate some fluctuation in salinity, although not to the extent of redfish and flounder, and can adapt to many types of habitat. They are most commonly found in inland bays and estuaries and beachfront waters but, at times, are found along the structure of nearshore oil platforms. They frequent grass flats, sand bars, shell reefs, and any other structure that attracts baitfish, provides ambush points and a break from strong currents.

Generally, speckled trout are most plentiful through summer months when they fill coastal bays to feed over structure. This, however, is not a rule without exceptions. There are bays that attract more fish during the dead of winter than at any other time. Likewise, there are areas rich with trout throughout the majority of spring and fishless in other seemingly prime periods.

Trout normally fill the bays and beachfronts in early spring to spawn and chase the brown shrimp crop as it exits the marsh and heads for the Gulf. Schools of trout take up residence over bay reefs, flats and channels and spend much of the summer there until the fall flush of white shrimp pulls many of them to the Gulf again.

There are many theories that point to two distinct strains of speckled trout occupying the bays and surf. Although there is no doubt there has to be strong interaction between the two strains, the possibility of genetically different subspecies within the trout population seems probable.

With wide mouths, sharp canine teeth, streamlined bodies, and eyes set high on their heads, speckled trout are built to chase prey. They have incredible vision and speed. If you have ever seen a trout chase a mullet across a clear flat, you will never again think it is possible to make a "too-fast" retrieve.

While smaller trout tend to school and hunt in packs, larger trout (6- to 10-pound fish) are often (though not exclusively) loners. Big schools of big trout do exist, but they are the exception.

Through early spring, many fish are on shorelines. As spawning abates and the heat of summer ensues, masses of trout move to mid-bay reefs and channels. Cooling temperatures and changes in baitfish patterns swell the reefs and shorelines with fish. Then winter's low tides and cold temperatures push fish out of the bays and concentrates the remaining straggler schools and loners. To be consistent, the speckled trout angler must adjust timing and tactics to these diverse patterns.

REDFISH

Sciaenops ocellata, red drum, channel bass, redfish and just plain "red" label this bulldog of the bays and nearshore waters. With hard, enamel-like scales, burly bone structure, slightly squared tail and weights approaching 100 pounds, nobody calls redfish lightweights. They are extremely adaptable to many conditions and can even survive in fresh water. They are dogged fighters and will eat everything from live baitfish to dead crab.

The delectable quality of redfish meat and a nation's demand for blackened redfish almost led to their extinction from overharvest. Commercial harvests in bay gill nets and Gulf purse seines decimated populations until the sweat, dollars and altruism of recreational anglers formed the GCCA which pushed the fisheries management system for proper conservation of this valuable resource.

The continued recovery of Gulf redfish populations has been a model for saltwater conservation programs across the nation. With literally millions of hatchery-produced redfish fingerlings stocked in coastal bays and sharp reductions in commercial fishing pressure, the redfish population has gone from the brink of disaster to a viable recreational game fish resource.

Redfish are not weak. They can adapt to extremely low salinity, and their senses allow them to feed adeptly by both sight and smell. Although their underslung mouths and low-set eyes drive them to root the bay and Gulf bottom for crabs, shrimp, sand worms and every other conceivable burrowing critter, an active redfish will readily chase a fleet-finned mullet or surface-crash a school of shad.

Reds are found in a variety of locations. From the

Jeff Davis with a back bay red.

PHOTO BY PAT MURRAY

backwaters of marsh canals and mud flats to the deep reefs and channels of bays, redfish are not habitat sensitive. Their hard shell of scales allows them to hug jetty rocks and barnacle-encrusted pilings.

Reds spend their early life in the bays and marshes but are called to the Gulf when they reach the 28-inch-plus range. During the Gulf storms of late summer and early fall, the surf and nearshore waters fill with schools of spawning redfish. This mating pattern is what made them so accessible to purse seine operations. Commercial fishermen could encircle large brood fish with nets and remove huge numbers of the spawning population in a single set.

Now coastal recreational anglers enjoy a primarily catch-and-release fishery for mature redfish. Although many states allow limited retention of mature fish, conscientious anglers release great numbers of these crucial spawners.

Redfish are highly gregarious, and schools can be immense. They sometimes surface in bays or the surf in a brass cloud of scales and tails.

From small to large, redfish present a great fight and superior table fare. Their abundance and diverse patterns make them accessible from Gulf piers to remote grass flats. Redfish are a true coastal treasure.

FLOUNDER

Paralichthys lethostigma, the southern flounder, is easily the oddest Texas coastal game fish. They begin life as any other fish, which means "bilateral" or having equal right and left sides and swim upright. As the fish mature, they go through a curious metamorphosis involving complex modification of the skeletal structure of the head and rearrangement of the nervous system and muscle tissues. As part of the changeover, the right eye migrates to the left side of the head and the fish spends its life laying on the bottom and swimming on its right side.

In other flounders, the left eye moves to the right side, but Gulf floun-der are "right-eyed" flounder.

The flounder family is immense. From the hotly contested fluke fishery of the Mid-Atlantic to the humble southern flounder of the Gulf, everyone likes flatfish. In fact, flounder are so popular, TPWD per-formed freshwater stocking experiments in the 1970s to make them available to inland fishermen. Unfortunately, though the fish lived in freshwater, they neither thrived nor reproduced and eventually disap-peared from the five stocking sites.

The flounder's incredibly strange body configuration makes it a true bottom-feeder but still a crafty predator. Its fantastic ability to cam-ouflage in the colors of the bay bottom and surprising speed allow it to clamp its razor-sharp teeth around shrimp, mullet, mud minnows, piggy perch, croaker, and anything else digestible.

Flounder have faced commercial pressure from gill nets, gigging and the indiscriminate drag of shrimp trawls. It is quite possible that the biggest drain on the flounder population in the Gulf is shrimp net by-catch. The implementation of regulations for by-catch reduction devices in some bays has helped, but much more needs to be done.

The flounder's life cycle makes it easy to pattern at certain times of the year. The annual fall spawning migration to the Gulf turns pass-es and channels into prime ambush points. Small male and large female "saddle blankets" cover bay shorelines adjacent to Gulf waters. They stream out of the bays, hugging the cover of jetty rocks, pilings and channel drop-offs. Flounder fishermen wait all year for this event. Dedicated anglers wade shorelines, dragging bait buckets full of hand-caught finger mullet and mud minnows, or comb the bottom with shad tails and curly tail jigs. Boat fishermen line deep channel edges and jetty passes, using fish-finder rigs to entice migrating flounder. For many, it is an event as anticipated as Christmas.

The flounder's feeding pattern is as strange as the fish's appearance.

It springs from the bottom to ambush its prey, and after capture, holds it in its cavernous mouth. It very slowly swallows whatever it has captured. This can present some maddening situations for anglers, particularly those who fish with lures. It is not uncommon to reel a flounder within inches of a net only to have it spit your offering back at your face. Without a doubt, flounder fishermen should always carry a net. Although it is no guarantee against an inadvertent quick release, it will help measurably. Losing a flounder at the net entails more than an empty spot on a stringer; the flesh is delectable, some say the best in the bay.

A fall flatfish – note the flounder's distended belly. It contained a four-inch-plus mullet.

PHOTO BY PAT MURRAY

Flounder return to the bays in spring and fill the deeper channels, shorelines and marsh through summer. Although not as concentrated as in fall, flounder can be caught around bay structure all year. By targeting hard structure, diehard flounder fishermen catch these tasty predators in almost all occasions.

As you can no doubt divine from this all-too-brief primer, a simultaneous assault on the Big Three takes study, dedication and no small amount of work. The rewards of a "bay slam" are well worth it.

Chapter Ten

Nearshore Tactics:
From tarpon to sharks, world class battles await within sight of coastal beaches

True titans of the Gulf lurk just beyond the breakers. To think that 150-pound tarpon, rooting bull reds, and swarms of blacktip, bull and the occasional hammerhead shark are within reach of coastal beaches is an almost unbelievable proposition. For swimmers, it is a sobering thought. For anglers, it is an exciting prospect.

The focus species for many nearshore big-game anglers has become the tarpon (a.k.a. "silver king"). They are an internationally revered and respected game fish that have become an object of pursuit for increasing numbers of Gulf coast anglers through the past decade.

The western Gulf has a sizable tarpon population. Although not a lot is known about their migratory patterns, they emerge along Texas coastal beaches through early summer and generally stay until the first significant cold front of early October. With great mysticism, they slip back into the warm currents of the Gulf and ease off to winter in more tropical destinations. For the few months they are here, they provide great sport and the opportunity for coastal anglers to catch a truly world-class fish within sight of land.

WHERE TO GO

Tarpon have an almost mystical hold on anglers. Part is based on the gargantuan leaps and dogged determination in battle, while part is their mysterious comings and goings in no readily decipherable pattern. Tremendous pods of tarpon can show up off a coastal beachfront or jetty overnight only to disappear just as quickly. Conversely, they can show up in a somewhat small location and fill the water column for months. "Unpredictable" is an understatement when it comes to the silver king, but to find them, you have to start somewhere.

PHOTO BY DOUG PIKE

A shark can be a welcomed sight on a slow day.

Capt. James Plaag and Capt. James Trimble of Silver King Adventures spend their summers chasing these elusive titans of the upper Texas coast. Both guides are quick to point out that finding the pods of tarpon is 80 percent of the battle.

"You can catch an occasional fish with blind luck," said Plaag. "But to establish a consistent pattern you have to put in the time and look for the fish."

Even with the transient nature of tarpon, there are places and times to begin your quest. Plaag suggested that one to three miles off the beach is a good starting point. Depths can fluctuate depending on what part of the coast you are fishing, but a good general depth is in the 20- to 40-foot range. For some perspective, three miles out from the mouth of San Luis Pass is approximately 30 feet deep.

Just as in all fishing, the first step to success is to pick proven spots to focus your search. San Luis Pass is legendary for its tarpon production through the years. As a Gulf pass, it is a mixing pot for bay and estuary outflow and hyper-saline Gulf currents. Located at the far west end of Galveston Island, the pass is best recognized from offshore by a huge, white water tower just east of the pass. Almost all significant Gulf passes offer the variable salinity and baitfish populations that attract tarpon. From Sabine Pass to Aransas Pass, Gulf breaks are always worth a look.

Gulf jetties add structure to the natural allure of any pass. These granite piers hold baitfish and help funnel bay outflows into nearby Gulf currents. The ends of jetties are prime starting points for tarpon seekers. It is not unusual for savvy rock-hoppers to run into an occasional silver king in the early and late summer.

River outflows offer direct input of nutrient-rich fresh or brackish water into the Gulf. They generally create sandbars at their mouths and hold large concentrations of mullet and menhaden through the summer months. These natural chum makers draw all varieties of Gulf-running game fish and are particularly appealing to the salinity-conscious coastal tarpon. In years of substantial freshwater outflow, Gulf river outlets can become beacons for tarpon.

WHAT TO LOOK FOR

It always surprises me that fishing tactics are almost the same regardless of species pursued. A blue marlin angler looks for baitfish, birds and slicks while trolling a distant oil platform, same as a trout fisherman drifting a bay reef.

Fish are fish, and anglers do well to remember it. Regardless of species, they all put their fins on one ray at a time. Tracking tarpon is no different than tracking trout. Both take patience and a good set of eyes.

"We look for slicks, baitfish, mud boils and, to a lesser degree, birds," said Trimble. "We use color lines, tide rips and occasionally fish around shrimp boats ("hot wagons"—see Glossary) that are culling their catch."

There is nothing arbitrary about tracking tarpon. It is a process of hours and days to find the signs necessary for locating them. Beachfront tarpon are transient in nature, but with the right combination of bait supply and water conditions, they may hold in given areas for weeks.

"We tend to find the larger schools in the same general areas year after year," said Plaag. "It may be clay or mud or something on the bottom that holds more shad or crabs, and the tarpon just naturally stay there longer. But we are using every sign we can until we find them."

Just as with bay trout fishing, slicks are the prime indicators for tarpon. The slicks may not necessarily indicate tarpon, but they almost always indicate some brand of feeding fish.

"It may be jacks or redfish or tarpon, but slicks are always a good sign, even in off-colored water," said Trimble. "We actually find a lot of our tarpon from slicks. They can be mixed with several other species all feeding on the same bait, but the key is seeing the signs to put you on the school."

GEARING UP FOR A PUNISHER

Had Yogi Berra been a tarpon fisherman, he might have said, "80 percent of tarpon fishing is finding them, and the other 80 percent is actually landing one."

Proper rigging for tarpon is critical for getting bites and having a chance of landing one. Unlike with shark, jackfish and kingfish, a half-hearted tarpon rig will usually end with a broken-hearted angler.

Most coastal fishing trips are measured by the number of fish landed. A tarpon trip is assayed by how many were jumped. The simple act of enticing and hooking one of these beasts can be reward enough for both experienced and amateur tarpon anglers. Actually landing one is a bonus.

Armed with 6-1/2-foot stand-up graphite fighting rods and Shimano TLD 15 reels spooled with 40-pound-test, Plaag and Trimble are ready to rumble.

"For drifting shad and ribbonfish, we use the stand-up tackle. With that gear, an experienced angler can whip a tarpon down fairly quickly," said Plaag. "But the real excitement is sight-casting plugs with 7-foot Castaway rods and Calcutta 400 reels."

If you want a big-time bite, imagine a 100-pound tarpon inhaling a MirrOLure in mid-retrieve. In September, when the conditions are calm and the tarpon are tightly schooled, it is not unusual to sight-cast to herds of tarpon within site of the Bolivar Beach sand.

In these situations, an electric trolling motor is a must. As tarpon roll and travel along the beach, a trolling motor allows anglers to intercept the schools without spooking them. The stealth of this approach also allows a greater ability to get the lure in front of the often-finicky fish. Plaag and Trimble's main picks for casting baits are 85M series MirrOLures in CHG (chartreuse belly and back with gold sides), HP (hot pink back and belly with silver sides) and 19 (green back with yellow belly).

They also use 2-ounce Coast Hawks, which are literally a painted piece of metal with two treble hooks. What the Coast Hawk lacks in human appeal it makes up for in tarpon appeal.

An equally unconventional go-to lure is the "Coon Pop." This Cajun import is basically a circle hook wired to a large, hookless jighead attached to an oversized curly tail jig. They can be cast but are primarily drifted. They help reduce unwanted shark hookups and can be used to cover the entire water column by drifting multiple lines at different depths.

Almost all casting lures are knotted to a 2- to 3-foot length of 80-pound-test leader. This helps against the rattling abrasion of gill plates without adversely affecting the plug's action.

When bait fishing, the standard practice involves rigging 100- to 150-pound-test monofilament leaders with 9/0 to 16/0 circle hooks and natural baits. The monofilament leaders are critical. Plaag and Trimble both agree that the keys to success are found in the swivel and loop knot.

"The rigging is very important. People need to use a high-quality, black, 100-pound-test Sampo swivel. That is very important, " said Plaag.

Trimble added, "The precision loop knot that attaches your hook is just as vital. The loop cannot slip and tighten around the hook. It is critical for the hookset to have that circle hook free-floating in the loop."

The devil is in the details, and tarpon are quick to find the devil in an angler's equipment. From shock leaders to fighting belts, you have to be prepared.

"You have to have the right gear," warned Plaag. "When we first started tarpon fishing years ago, we lost a lot of fish due to equipment failures. If you do not use the right stuff, you're simply going to lose fish."

WHEN ROUGH IS TOO ROUGH

If you wait for perfect conditions, you will likely never go fishing.

Flat, calm days are the exception, but to find tarpon, calmer is better.

"You can catch fish in some pretty rough stuff, but finding fish in that stuff is really hard," said Plaag. "If you are on them, 4- to 6-foot seas are not impossible. But it is hard to see any fish signs when you can hardly stand up in the boat."

Using up-to-the-minute information acces-

The unmistakably stubborn look of a jackfish.

PHOTO BY DOUG PIKE

sible via the Internet, the best advice is to watch the buoy reports and surf cams to get a real-time view of the beach. This will allow you to judge the value and, more importantly, safety of your time on the water.

ALTERNATIVE SPECIES: WHEN THE KING HAS LEFT THE BUILDING

Alternative bay species can break up a slow fishing session. Alternative species off the beachfront can absolutely wear you out. With an abundance of sharks, jackfish, kingfish and redfish stalking nearshore waters, the alternatives to fickle tarpon can be more inviting that the silver king itself.

When the tarpon are elusive, a fast trip to a culling shrimp boat can often result in quick hookups and acceptable table fare. Try free-lining a shad or ribbonfish in the free chum line and hold on to your gear.

Nearshore oil platforms and standpipes are great structure that hold a variety of nearshore species. Jackfish, sharks and occasional ling will cruise platforms and pipes and are a great diversion on a slow-bite day.

June and July are prime months to catch large king mackerel surprisingly close to shore on drifted ribbonfish. Late summer and early fall ushers in the redfish spawn and attendant "bull red run." Sharks are omnipresent and almost always offer a willing mouth, but remember that nothing is 100 percent.

Believe it or not, there are days when nothing will bite, just like in the finicky world of bay fishing. Some days, the Gulf seems just plain dead.

SAVE MONEY, HIRE A GUIDE

Tarpon fishing can be very complicated. From rigging techniques to interpreting dangerous weather patterns, a day even a little way from shore can quickly turn into a disaster. There is always value in recruiting the help of a pro when beginning any pursuit, but in tarpon fishing, it is almost a must.

From golf lessons to tarpon fishing, hiring a pro can help accelerate the learning curve and teach a beginner if it is the right sport for him or not. For those who fall in love with nearshore tarpon fishing, the dog days of summer cannot come soon enough, but if that is not your game, it is best to learn before investing the time, money and effort.

Chapter Eleven

Alternate Species:
The fish We Love to Hate

We all knew them or maybe even were them—the last kids picked for the dodgeball team. It was not always a fair assessment. Maybe it was because they were inferred to be smaller or weaker or some other superficial inferiority. They were not the A-team. They may have gone on to be Olympic champs, but at that time, they were not Bo Jackson.

This same scenario is played out on our coastal bays every day. After the speckled trout, redfish and flounder have been picked over, many coastal anglers' interest begins to fade. When times get tough, alternative species can turn a horror show into an award winner. With a little variation in game plan and technique, these character actors can provide a diversion from the fickle habits and tastes of the prima donnas and Oscar winners of the bay.

SHEEPSHEAD

The largest member of the American porgies, the sheepshead is a common customer to almost any barnacle-encrusted bay structure. From pier pilings to jetty rocks, the convict fish (so named for its tell-tale prison-stripe markings) is easily accessible to boat and shore-bound anglers alike.

They are not overly picky about feeding times. It is common to see them grazing along jetty rocks through the middle of the day even in the most inhospitable tide and water temperature. Their thick lips and almost human-looking teeth allow them to snip barnacle off virtually any structure and smash any protective shell of an unassuming crustacean or mollusk.

Five- and six-pound sheepshead are not uncommon, and larger specimens are currently swimming around the pilings, rocks and docks of our coast. They provide a very sporty fight. With a broad side and powerful body structure, a sheepshead will test conventional trout tackle. For those willing to test their fillet knife against sharp dorsal spikes and armor-like scales, the sheepshead has a mild, white meat meshed in endless ribs. The one good thing about their formidable bone structure is that there are very few sneaky bones; most are easily seen and removed.

Sheepshead are very abundant and accessible along most coastal jetties. During winter, crowds of anglers with modified cane poles dip short leads of heavy monofilament around the granite washouts. Using a small single or treble hook tipped with a small fiddler crab, sand flea, sea roach or small piece of peeled dead shrimp, they adeptly probe the edges of submerged rocks for burly convicts. This same strategy can be applied with conventional casting tackle from the rocks or well-positioned boat. The key is getting a small offering directly in the teeth of the structure. Sheepshead will not stray far from this private buffet. Their armored skin allows close contact with rough structure.

You will need a solid stretch of 25-pound test leader to avoid break-offs, and even with that protection, remember to periodically check for nicks and abrasion. With a disproportionately small mouth, sheepshead require a small No. 8 or 10 treble or equally small single hook. Even this tough hardware requires constant inspection. Punishment from abrasive rocks and the clamp-like jaws of the sheepshead means hooks seldom stay in top condition.

Sheepshead anglers are the only coastal recreationalists other than clam diggers whose equipment list includes a long-handled shovel. Through years of being a bit of a jetty rat, I watched experienced sheepshead assassins walk the jetty with their shovels. They would setup their fishing gear, walk to the edge of a cluster of rocks, and begin scraping barnacles into the water. As the barnacle bits float down the rocks, they attract and concentrate grazing sheepshead. The angler then prepares his equipment and focuses his effort on the chummed area. Believe me, it really works. They may not be pretty or the subject of magazine pictorials, but a few sheepshead can make a gem out of a no-bite day.

SPANISH MACKEREL

Spanish mackerel can provide a great diversion for struggling trout fishermen during the dog days of summer. They are plentiful around beachfront piers and jetties and are accessible by boat and shore. They often school and incite large flocks of gulls and terns as they push shad, shrimp and anything that gets in front of their teeth to the surface. The action can be fast and easy, but remember to bring some piano wire leaders and black swivels.

Mackerel have razor sharp teeth that easily melt through light monofilament. Unless you luck out and hook one in the corner of the mouth, a leader is a must. Although black swivels are a hedge against alerting sharp game fish eyes, in the case of a mackerel, the color is critical. In the melee of an actively feeding school, the flash and bubble of a fast-moving brass or stainless steel swivel will often incite a line-cutting strike from an eager mack.

With an average weight in the 2- to 4-pound range, mackerel are a good match with trout tackle. They feed on a host of baitfish ranging from glass minnows to shrimp. In a feeding frenzy, anything that flashes is fair game.

A 1/4- to 1/2-ounce silver or silver/chartreuse spoon is a prime lure for macks. It can be cast from a pier or jetty and even slow trolled behind a boat around the ends of jet-

Spanish mackerel

ties. Macks generally respond to a fast retrieve, but if they are suspended fairly deep, a slower retrieve may be required.

For the natural bait fishermen, a free-lined live shrimp or shad is a good call. Try adding a red bead above the hook. The added color makes the bait stand out from its surroundings.

Spanish mackerel mavens shudder at the notion of categorizing macks as an "alternative" species. Properly prepared, mackerel is a gastronomic delight. Speedy runs and an aggressive demeanor make them a fine game fish. The next time the Gulf flattens and the bay bite stops, go slow troll a spoon or look for a beachfront flock of birds. You may find a new favorite fish.

SAND TROUT

The sand trout is the ignored and often beleaguered relative of the speckled trout. At times, they can actually become annoying to speckled trout anglers. They fill bay reefs during summer and gobble every shrimp or jig that hits the water. When the Big Three seem to develop lockjaw, sand trout can save the day.

Sand trout are eclectic in their dietary habits. They readily accept a small jig and are suckers for a small piece of peeled dead shrimp. Even in the worst of dog-day summers, it is possible to coax a bite from a sandy with a bit of shrimp offered on a lightweight fish-finder rig. They are a great "starter fish" for youngsters and put up a surprisingly good fight. Larger specimens of up to 15 inches or more can fool the most savvy speckled trout angler for the first few seconds of the fight.

The sand trout's table qualities are grossly underrated. If prepared fresh, they rival speckled trout. Their filets can be preserved if frozen in water, but do not expect the same quality of meat when defrosted. The best thing to do with leftover fillets is use them to make stock for gumbo, fish chowder or bouillabaisse. The sweet, soft meat adds a unique taste and texture.

The Big Three are under no threat of becoming the Big Four from the humble sand trout. Nonetheless, when the going gets tough, more than a few anglers and guides (and ex-guides) have sheepishly made a day with a box of sand trout and will continue to do so.

We have barely scratched the surface of the staggering diversity of species the Gulf has to offer. Black drum, skipjack, jack crevalle, croaker, and sharks are just a few of the possibilities. From food fish to fighters, there are plenty of species to target as long as you do not let your focus get too narrow. Keep an open mind, and your days of getting skunked could be over forever.

Black drum are among the other "alternate species" offered by Gulf waters.

Chapter Twelve

Landlocked:
A guide to quality fishing without a boat

Just because you do not have a boat does not mean you cannot enjoy quality coastal fishing. Shoreline privatization, channels, canals and the Intracoastal Waterway have bottled up a great deal of shore-bound fishing opportunities, but by utilizing public piers, jetties, and shoreline and marsh wade-fishing spots, you can fish the coast without feeling handicapped.

BETTER WITHOUT A BOAT

There are times when certain spots are simply better fished without a boat. I firmly believe it is better to fish the beachfront out of a truck rather than a boat. By walking or driving the beach you have a better perspective to see fish signs. It is much easier to see slicks, jumping mullet and other signs looking out from the sand. When running the beachfront in a boat, you lose much of the needed perspective to read the inside bars.

Rock-walkers can also have a great advantage over boaters when fishing jetties. The rock walker has better mobility to move up and down the rocks without having to deal with anchors, tide and adverse

wind. The rock-hopper can fish a spot for a few casts and simply move on to another rock. If you catch a fish, you can setup camp without drifting off the sweet spot.

The best example of walk-in waders having the advantage is along the Dollar Flats at Texas City. A storm-containment levee towers over these productive sand flats. As you drive down the levee road, you can see clearly across the entire body of the flat. Any mullet, slicks or color changes stand out like hot-pink neon. It is an incredible advantage over the limited perspective from a boat deck.

TIGHTEN YOUR FOCUS

Walk-in wade-fishing has a number of distinct advantages, not the least of which is narrowed focus. You almost have to look at the shoreline or cove that you are fishing as a self-contained lake. It is a limited amount of fishing space, and you have to decipher the pattern in that little world. To an extent, what lies beyond the pass is irrelevant.

Lack of options can be a great motivating factor, necessity being a mother and all. There have been countless times over the years that I drove a great distance to the Anahuac Wildlife Refuge only to be disappointed by poor water quality, lack of baitfish, tough bite or an adverse wind. On the other hand, I can equally recount some phenomenal trips that came about because I had nowhere else to go. I stuck it out and tried to make the best of the situation. Through this, I learned to catch more fish in seemingly unfishable conditions.

The almost limitless possibilities of a boat can actually work against you. It is easy to give up on a spot and run the whole day looking for the textbook shoreline that may not exist. A shore-bound angler picks his spot and concentrates on the details free of the temptation to see what lies miles down the shore. His sharpened focus allows him to see subtleties that a boated angler might miss, and he finds the lemonade hidden in a field of lemons.

HAVE MORE THAN ONE ARROW IN YOUR QUIVER

The cardinal rule if you are going somewhere is that you have to have someplace to go. You must have a spot for almost any conditions. A good landlocked angler can make an art of it. Always interpret the elements with an eye toward selecting a spot that offers the best wind protection, structure and tide for the ambient conditions. You have to have a spot for every wind direction and season.

Always be on the lookout for new spots. Part of the fun of fishing without a boat is finding new spots. Just like a boat angler, you have to figure a route to the spot, read the water and decipher the conditions that determine the best way and time to fish it.

GET READY TO RUMBLE

Pier and jetty anglers have the luxury of lugging in as much extra gear as they want—within reason, anyway. Carts and wagons provide a conveyance for much-needed extra baits, reels, drinks and all the small amenities that make for an enjoyable trip.

A walk-in wader is often a long distance from the vehicle that got him there, so proper gear selection and packing is important. I always follow the philosophy that less is more, but if you are going to make a day on a shoreline, it is necessary to bring more than the usual small selection of terminal tackle.

If you have limited space to fish and thus limited schools of fish to access, you need to have a large variety of baits. Stick to the usual major food groups in natural and artificial baits, just increase the quantity. Bring more colors and styles of lures or a larger quantity of live or dead baits and the necessary rigging material.

Having plenty to drink is crucial to extend the life of your trip. Most anglers do not realize how much water they lose through sweat, even in cool weather. Having a cool drink available is both comforting and necessary. Try putting one or two canned drinks or bottled water in neoprene can holders and place them in a belt bag. They will stay relatively cool for some time and remain out of your way until needed.

KAYAKS

Kayaks have been around for a long time but hit mainstream saltwater angling only in the last few years. They come in a variety of shapes and sizes and are easily transported in small trucks and SUVs. They have opened up a new world of shallow-water access to coastal anglers, allowing increased mobility without the cost and trouble of larger boats. The kayak obviously cannot match the range of even a small outboard-powered boat, but it offers increased access and stealth at a reasonable price.

WHERE TO GO

Here, let us examine a few of the better bank fishing locations with an eye to creating a starter library of spots for all occasions. As with most walk-in spots, these are not secrets by any stretch of the imagination, but like all fishing spots, it is a matter of timing, reading the water and using the right techniques that produces fish.

ANAHUAC WILDLIFE REFUGE

This is the best walk-in wading spot I know. It is undoubtedly the best location to catch a trophy trout on the upper coast, and it consistently produces fish year-around.

The refuge has substantial marsh inflows from Oyster Bayou, Robinson's Bayou, and a series of smaller tributary marsh canals and rainwater ditches that feed its shoreline. The majority of the shoreline is mud with scattered stretches of shell and some firmer

PHOTO BY PAT MURRAY

Louis McAfee with a limit of Anahuac Refuge reds.

sandy areas.

The refuge's remote location in the far east end of Galveston's East Bay makes it both rich with natural habitat and frequently void of crowds.

There are two main access roads that lead to the bay. Both drop you into prime wade-fishing areas. To be honest, there really is not a bad spot along the refuge shoreline. Except for the thick, deep mud around Frozen Point, the bay bottom is fairly forgiving for even an inexperienced wader.

The elements influencing good water clarity on this shoreline are an east, northeast, or north wind and no substantial freshwater run off from Oyster Bayou. Surprisingly, the hook of Frozen Point provides protection even in a fairly stout east wind and holds fishable water in adverse conditions.

A large tide is a must. Low water is a recipe for disaster in this back bay location. Try to time your wade around a large incoming tide. Any east in the wind will help augment the tide and, subsequently, help your wade.

On a big tide, look for redfish tight against the shoreline cord grass. Remember to zigzag the shoreline and focus on baitfish. If the mullet are shallow, fish shallow. If the bait is deep, go to it. The bait will usually tell you where the fish are. Also remember that this is a great topwater spot.

The refuge is located east of Houston. Take I-10 east, take the Hankamer exit (Hwy. 61) and go right. Go straight until the road forks and veer to the left onto 1985. It will take you to the refuge entrance, which will be on your right. Sign in at the registration station and look at the refuge map to get oriented. Remember bug spray and keep your eyes peeled for local wildlife.

DOLLAR FLATS

To this day, the largest 10-fish limit of trout I ever caught came from a walk-in trip at Dollar Flats. Located on the western shoreline of Lower Galveston Bay, this industrialized shoreline can produce outstanding fishing in spring, summer and fall.

With close access to the Houston Ship Channel, it receives substantial Gulf flow and is a great spot during years of significant freshwater inflow. As mentioned in the introduction of this chapter, the levee that protects Texas City serves as a great lookout for surveying this hardsand shoreline.

The best spot is approximately 1/2 to one mile down the levee road. There is a ridge where the sand flat drops off and gradually arcs away from the rocks bordering the shoreline. It stretches out toward the ship channel and creates a great wading flat that is covered with trout through spring and summer.

As you drive the levee, look for lines of mullet and slicks. Do not be afraid to put in a long wade on this shoreline. When you get tired, just wade to shore, scale the rocks and walk back to your vehicle. Be careful entering and exiting the water. The rocks that protect the shoreline can be slippery and treacherous.

This is a great shoreline for all kinds of wade-fishing, from bait soaking to walking a topwater. There are no limits.

An added bonus at this spot is the variety of nearby options. The levee road takes you to Dollar Point at the base of Dollar Reef and the spillway that protects Moses Lake. Both spots are worth a try.

The mouth of Moses Lake is a popular night fishing spot. As you might imagine, an outgoing tide from this marsh-rich lake can empty multitudes of trout, redfish and flounder through the relatively small spillway opening.

Dollar Flats is generally best on an incoming tide while the Moses Lake spillway and its adjacent flats are great on an outgoing flow.

PHOTO BY PAT MURRAY

The author with a string of walk-in trout.

The levee provides a great edge against south, southwest, west and somewhat against northwest winds. The key thing to remember is that the Dollar flats can provide fishable conditions even with a nagging southwest wind.

These spots are accessible by taking I-45 south to the Texas City exit (Hwy. 1764 east). Exit and cross over the freeway. This road will take you through town and eventually ends at a T in the road. Take a right at the stop sign and an almost immediate left at the stoplight. Get on the Texas City Dike and take a left at the stop sign on the ridge of the levee. This puts you on the levee road.

SAN LUIS PASS

Legends have been made at Gulf passes. Anything is possible where the Gulf meets the bay. Tarpon roll, trout school—and you never know what your next bite will be.

San Luis Pass is bordered on the Gulf and bay side by productive sand flats. It provides particularly good fishing in spring and summer, but wind and tide are critical to success around the pass. If the wind is light and the surf is green, it is hard to beat wading the beach-front east of the pass. The guts and bars of the surf become highways for all types of game fish and offer a great walk-in option. Beware of strong tides. Anglers die every year by not wearing a life jacket and not paying attention to the strength of the tide. The closer you get to the pass, the stronger the current.

The bayside east of the pass provides a great option if the wind has muddied the surf. With a southeast or east wind and incoming tide, these flats provide easy wade-fishing for trout. This area produces numbers of limits through the year and is a great early morning or late afternoon topwater spot. You may not catch as many with a topwater, but they will usually be trout that make you proud.

The pass is located on the far west end of Galveston Island and can be accessed by taking I-45 south and exiting at 61st Street. Go right on 61st and take it to the seawall. Go right and drive the seawall to the end of the island. You will see the surf on your left and bay coves to your right.

BAYCLIFF SPILLWAY

The Baycliff Spillway dumps warm water into the bay from the nearby power plant. Warm currents draw fish from the adjacent Seabrook and Kemah Flats and hold sizable numbers of fish through fall and winter.

The spillway is productive both day and night. It is a popular spot for train-light fishermen and has a public pier that offers night fishing under lights.

During the day, fishing the spillway outflow can be great. It is like fishing a fast-moving river. The banks are covered with rocks to protect against erosion. This makes fishing the bank treacherous and has led to a build up of tackle-stealing rocks within casting range. The key is casting toward the middle of the outflow and letting your bait go with the flow. Most bites are near the bottom so heavier jigheads and weights are necessary.

The deep channel of the outflow mandates a slip-cork or fish-finder rig. When using a slip cork, try experimenting with the depth between eight and 12 feet until you find the strike zone. With a fish-finder rig, start out with a 1/2-ounce egg sinker, increasing or lessening weight as the current dictates.

Use 1/4- to 3/8-ounce jigheads to get soft plastics through the current. Stick with red shad and pumpkinseed Bass Assassins and dark colored shad tails. Expect some hang-ups but also expect some fish.

The spillway provides protection under southeast, south and somewhat with a southwest wind.

Spillway outflow greatly impacts the tide. It is usually best on an incoming tide, but the velocity and heat of the outflow is the most influential factor.

The spillway is located just off Hwy. 646. Take I-45 south and exit at Hwy. 646. Go toward Baycliff (there is a sign) until the road meets the bay. Turn right and follow the road to Spillway Park. Remember to check out the flats adjacent to the spillway. They can offer some great wade-fishing opportunities year-around.

CHRISTMAS BAY

Located on the west side of San Luis Pass, Christmas Bay offers some of the most pristine walk-in wade-fishing along the entire coast. With sea grass, shell reefs and shoreline guts within walking distance of the road, it is a rare opportunity for boatless anglers.

Christmas Bay is known for its trout, flounder and redfish. It is a frequent stalking spot for fly-fishermen and has produced enough trophy trout to put it in an elite category.

As with many shoreline spots, a high tide is best. A flooding high tide pushes baitfish onto the bank and pours Gulf inflow into the bay.

Christmas Bay is at its best during spring and fall. As trout are preparing to spawn, they frequent the bay's protected, habitat-rich shorelines. During fall, much of the bay's abundant baitfish and shrimp populations move to the Gulf and cover the shell, grass and mud of the south shoreline on the journey. A southeast or south wind is best on this shoreline.

Christmas Bay is on the west side of the San Luis Pass Bridge. By following the main access road off the west end of the Island, you see Christmas on your right after exiting the bridge.

"Landlocked" is not a negative term. It suggests restricted access, but that is not necessarily a bad thing. In an era of over-

Landlocked does not mean "not getting' 'em."

powered boats, many anglers drive past the best spots to fish.

With miles of beachfront, jetties, beach and bay piers, and a large selection of public shorelines, the coast provides a lot of opportunity for boatless anglers.

A fishing spot is what you make it. Almost every spot has some fish at some time. The keys are figuring out when they are there and how to catch them. By having to focus on a limited set of spots, you address those locations with greater concentration and effort, and that is what leads to better catches.

PHOTO BY PAT MURRAY

"Now that was a blow up..."

Chapter
Thirteen

Texas' Five Hottest bays

THE HOTTEST SPOTS NOW AND FOR THE FUTURE

In writing this chapter, I decided to dissect five specific bays along the Texas coast that will likely be prime producers through the coming years. This was not an easy decision. Establishing criteria to support and assure the accuracy of such prognostication was not easy.

First off, I selected candidates based on ease of access and therefore, subject to more or less fishing pressure. The second factor was strength and viability of the fishery and the likelihood it would continue producing numbers and quality in the future. Finally, I gauged the impact of fishing pressure, habitat degradation and natural anomalies (red and brown tides and freezes).

Picking the best five bays for the coming millennium is about as exact a science as picking the top five stocks for the next 100 years. Both necessarily involve significant guesswork. The one thing I can guarantee is that my picks will not make you go broke.

Although the other contestants fit the criteria and are most certainly possessed of poise and beauty (and don't look bad in a swimsuit, either), the winners are: Sabine Lake, Galveston's East Bay, Galveston's West Bay, East Matagorda Bay, and Rockport.

Each of these bays possess distinct characteristics that make them unique. Varying amounts of freshwater inflow, Gulf access, natural marsh, local habitat, and fishing pressure are but a few of the variables that aggregate each bay's individual "personality."

All of these bays are reasonably accessible and sport adequate facilities from lodging to boat ramps. They all have great track records for producing trophy fish and quantities of fish, have stable or recovering habitat, and solid prospects to sustain current levels or even improve in the coming decades.

Like so much of this book, this chapter is a personal journal. It is a look at specific spots and how to address them. After years of guiding and speaking to anglers at seminars, I have learned that discussing fishing theory and strategy is not nearly as satisfying or exciting as detailing exact spots right down to the last oyster shell.

I picked these particular locations because I believe they will help people catch more fish. Locale alone will not make anyone a better fisherman, but combined with correctly reading signs, proper wading and drifting techniques, and appropriate lure or natural bait methods, these spots serve as wide-open portals to the treasures we all seek.

SABINE LAKE

Sabine Lake is no longer a secret. Outside of its legendary south end drift-fishing and occasional rumor of teaming flocks of gulls over keeper trout, it remained out of the mainstream angling focus until the past five years. Finally, stories of 60-pound limit stringers of trout from the Louisiana shoreline and monster trout grenading topwaters thrown from a drifting boat in 6 feet of water proved to be too much. I was lured there during the 1999 Troutmasters Classic and saw a remarkable

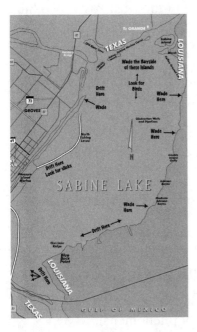

Sabine Color Map, page C/10

majority of the Top Ten stringers come from the upper end of the lake; they were not average fish. Four pounds average was, well, just average.

Sabine is unique in the abundant freshwater inflow from its north end and direct Gulf influence from Sabine Pass. It has a spectacular collection of mountainous shell reefs in the south end and an unparalleled estuary on the eastern shore. With speculation that the next Texas or Louisiana state record trout could come from this relatively small body of water, the crowds are unlikely to disperse anytime soon. With so much habitat and a unique balance of marsh and Gulf influence, Sabine Lake is likely to be a prime bay for a very long time to come.

When the drift-fishing bite at the south end gets hot, the crowds rival anything Galveston can muster. Hundreds of boats drift the deep mounds of shell. The unique thing is that most anglers do not throw their baits in front of the drift. Instead, they throw worm-like soft plastics on heavy jigheads behind their boat and let the natural flow of the drift move the bait. Some anglers actually rig their boats to drift multiple rods in holders and sit back to watch for bites, a technique not unlike trolling. It is fascinating to watch and somewhat boring to do, but when the bite is happening, it can be a kick.

Trout typically come into the lake through the pass to feed on shrimp and shad exiting the lake's substantial marsh. Long time Sabine angler Fred Miller points out that a general lineup for this pattern is easy.

"By setting up drifts on either side of the Goal Posts [two huge pilings roughly in the middle of the south end of the lake], you can cut long drifts and cover a lot of shell."

When shrimp fill the bay in spring and fall, trout and redfish action under birds is fantastic. Cruise the middle of the lake when conditions allow and watch for surfacing trout and reds chasing bait. Miller said when this is happening, "It is big-time action like you cannot imagine."

With a blooming estuary on one side and the riches of the Gulf on the other, Sabine presents a dichotomy. For anglers, these two faces of the lake present distinct patterns to unravel. The jetties are legendary. One of the most reliable redfish patterns is at the ends of these rock piers. During an outgoing tide, deep washouts at the jetty tips produce redfish action that is nothing short of phenomenal.

"No matter what you fish, natural or artificial, it takes some weight to get it through the current and to the fish in these washouts," said Miller. "I prefer a glow with chartreuse tail and generally use a 3/8- to 1/2-ounce jighead."

Like all jetties, a trolling motor and topwater bait produces memorable action, but few rock piles can match Sabine. It is, in a word, breathtaking. In southwest or light wind, try the base of the Gulf side of the northern jetty. It creates a flat similar to the Bolivar Pocket that is as near perfect for wading and drifting as you are likely to find.

During the heavy heat of summer, the nearshore rigs on the Louisiana side of the rocks offer a great deep-water alternative. Many rigs are just a mile or two from the beach, but remember that they are in Louisiana waters and that state's regulations apply. Live bait anglers and lure fishermen utilize this structure to target trout along the pilings and additional structures that surround these platforms. The key is to fish all around the rig structure until you locate a school. This can define the pattern for most of the neighboring platforms as well.

The north end of the lake is typified by marsh inflow and estuary influence. The three islands on the north shoreline—Goat, Stewts and Sydnes—are bordered by the Intracoastal Canal and the main body of the bay. Each spoil island provides topography suitable for wade- and drift-fishermen. Most waders target the points of the islands. To properly target a drift, parallel the islands and focus on the many channels and depressions created by the spoil. Prime baits are Bass Assassin, topwaters and, if necessary, live bait.

Coffee Ground Cove has achieved legendary status for producing big trout for both waders and drifters. With a prolific estuary feeding the cove, it is no wonder that it teams with all links of the food chain. The northern tip of the cove juts into the bay and produces a natural flat for baitfish and hungry game fish.

"This flat can produce some of the most phenomenal topwater fishing on the lake," said Miller.

The east side of the lake is riddled with bayou mouths and marsh sloughs. Every estuary output is a potential drifting target. As tides fall out of these brackish lifelines, they pump baitfish and game fish into the bay. During fall, this pattern is at its best. Key on baitfish activity and work the outside of any visible connection to the marsh.

In describing Sabine Lake, you cannot neglect the exceptional flounder fishing. There are anglers who live for the fall flounder migration. Every eastside bayou mouth just screams "Flounder here!" With an unending flow of minnows, mud fish and shrimp, flounder take station on the points outside bayou mouths to ambush passing baitfish. With Sabine's record for producing trophy-caliber trout, it is hard to imagine giving up prime topwater time for dabbling a jig for a flatfish, but when push comes to shove, it is hard to pass up the creative finesse it takes to coax a lurking flounder; the table fare is worth its weight in trout.

Sabine Lake only recently caught the general public's eye. Its crowds could begin to abate, and it may well slip back into some degree of obscurity in the shadow of East Matagorda or Baffin Bay. Be that as it may, if I had to place a bet on the water body that will produce the next 13-pound-plus trout, my money would be squarely on Sabine's nose. Time will tell.

EAST GALVESTON BAY

If there is any one bay that I would call home, it is Galveston's East Bay, despite the fact that I live on West Bay. It sits in the far northeast corner of the bay system and has some of the richest marsh in the entire complex. I believe East Bay supports the largest redfish population in the system,

East Bay Color Map, page C/12

although some would argue that Trinity Bay holds more. It sports a very large collection of productive live shell reefs. The shorelines are typified by sand and mud with periodic shell clusters. There is no bay-bottom sea grass, but there is ample shoreline cord grass. Almost the entire north shoreline is undeveloped and still reaps the benefits of unfettered marsh inflow. East Bay supports a healthy marsh ecosystem with the sprawling canals, bayous and mudflats of Marsh Point and the protected Anahuac Wildlife Refuge.

It enjoys tremendous Gulf inflow from Galveston Pass and flow from the Houston Ship Channel. It weathers substantial fishing pressure from Houston but still manages to be a tournament favorite for any

Galveston Bay Complex event. East Bay may not be virgin, but what it lacks in purity, it makes up for in rich marsh and blooming oysters.

The dredging of the Houston Ship Channel in the late 1990s and into this century was thought to be a death sentence for East Bay. I thought the so-called "wetland restoration" would be nothing more than a euphemism for "spoil dump." I was wrong. For the most part, the structure created by the dredging process has actually created viable spawning aggregation areas and recreational fishing spots. Although the long-term ramifications are unknown, this project appears to have not destroyed the heritage of East Bay anglers.

East Bay runs on a northeast/southwest axis and provides at least some protected water under most conditions. For wade-fishermen, it is rare to not find somewhere to hide from adverse weather and catch fish. Throughout much of the year, mid-bay reefs offer almost unlimited drift-fishing opportunities.

Siever's Cut opens the Intracoastal Waterway (ICW) to the west end of the bay. It has hard, current-influenced shorelines on both sides of the cut. The western bank is very steep. It has a shell point where it meets the ICW and transitions to sand as it cuts back to the west, creating the north face of Goat Island. It lacks the deep guts and bars that are synonymous with much of the shoreline but serves as a great spring and summer wade-fishing spot. With occasional small schools of redfish tight against the bank and outstanding trout fishing along the drop-off, this shoreline has produced winning stringers for several tournaments; my 1995 Guide's Cup victory came from this spot.

The eastern bank, called "the Bluff," has a small shell point where it cuts from the ICW. Like the western bank, it can provide some redfish action but is primarily a trout spot. During fall, both banks produce tremendous flounder catches for those willing to drag mud minnows and finger mullet around this manmade bay pass.

One of the true secrets of these spots is their ability to produce trout action even during a dead tide. When the trout bite abates in neighboring areas, try wading the banks just outside the ICW. The ebb and flow of near-constant barge traffic creates an artificial tide that can stimulate a bite. Do not hesitate to throw topwaters through the middle of the day even in the heat of summer. The proximity of the shoreline to the depths of the Intracoastal seems to make trout immune to sum-mer dog-day patterns.

Pepper Cove is one of the few true coves in East Bay. It receives a lot of pressure, for good reason. It has a distinct shell reef on its west-ern point and a solid patch of shell in the back end. It benefits from a marsh inlet to Elm Lake, a rarely-fished redfish hotspot on the east side of the cove. Pepper Cove is often best on a strong incoming tide. As the tide rips in, it sweeps trout across the outside shell point while creating prime spawning conditions in the back of the cove.

On a high tide, try drifting or wading Elm Lake for redfish, the latter only if you are mud savvy. Pepper Cove is best for trout in spring and fall and is a favorite of fall flatfish anglers.

Elmgrove Point has always been a no-man's land. Its deep, clay-lined shoreline and periodic marsh outlets do not present a particular-ly appealing landscape. Nonetheless, in spring, schools of trout travel this bank as they push back into the bay to spend the summer on mid-bay reefs. This deep-bank wade is not for the impatient. It takes long, deep wades that invariably fill your waders and wear out your arms. The payoff is tremendous trout catches even in screaming, springtime southeast winds. It usually takes finesse baits to pattern these fish. A 7M series MirrOLure or jerkworm with a light head entices these transient fish.

Fat Rat Pass is the Disney World of fishing: Long lines, big crowds but still a lot of fun. Everyone knows Fat Rat. It is a large, bar-

PHOTO BY PAT MURRAY

TREASURE MAPS

Texas' Five Hottest Bays

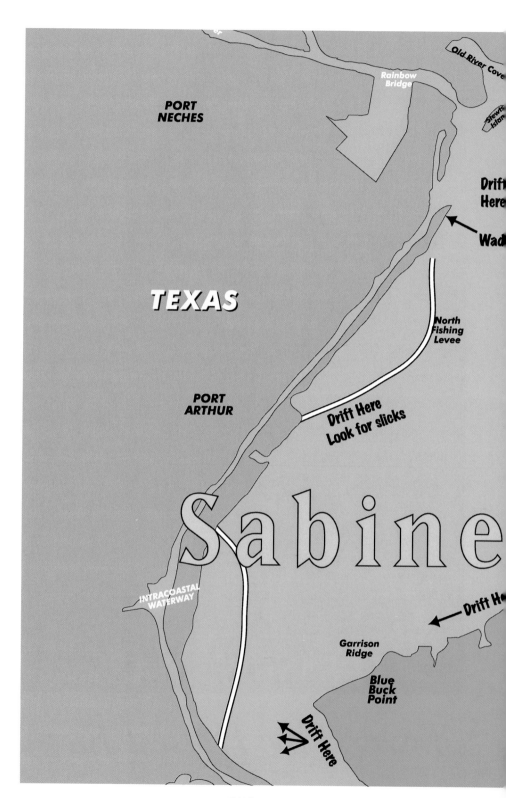

Old River Cove

Rainbow
Bridge

**PORT
NECHES**

Drift
Here

Wade

TEXAS

North
Fishing
Levee

**PORT
ARTHUR**

Drift Here
Look for slicks

Sabine

INTRACOASTAL
WATERWAY

Drift He

Garrison
Ridge

Blue
Buck
Point

Drift Here

Neches Canal

Sabine
Island

Marsh

Wade the Bayside
of these Islands

Coffee Ground Cove

Drift
Here

Wade
Here

Look for
Birds

Wade
Here

LOUISIANA

Obstruction Wells
and Pipelines

Wade
Here

N

Double
Island
Gully

Johnson
Bayou

Madame
Johnson
Bayou

Lake

Wade
Here

LOUISIANA

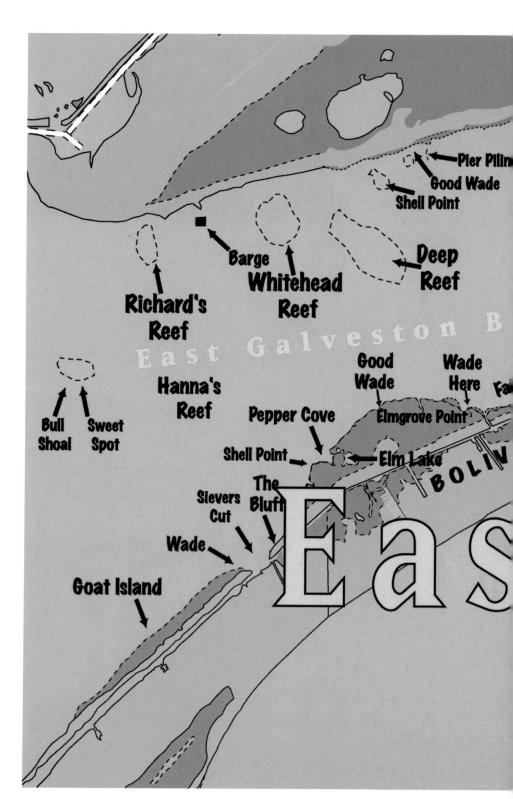

Pier Pilin
Good Wade
Shell Point

Barge
Whitehead Reef

Deep Reef

Richard's Reef

East Galveston B

Good Wade

Wade Here

Fa

Bull Shoal   Sweet Spot

Hanna's Reef

Pepper Cove

Elmgrove Point

Shell Point

Elm Lake

BOLIV

The Bluff

Sievers Cut

Eas

Wade

Goat Island

East

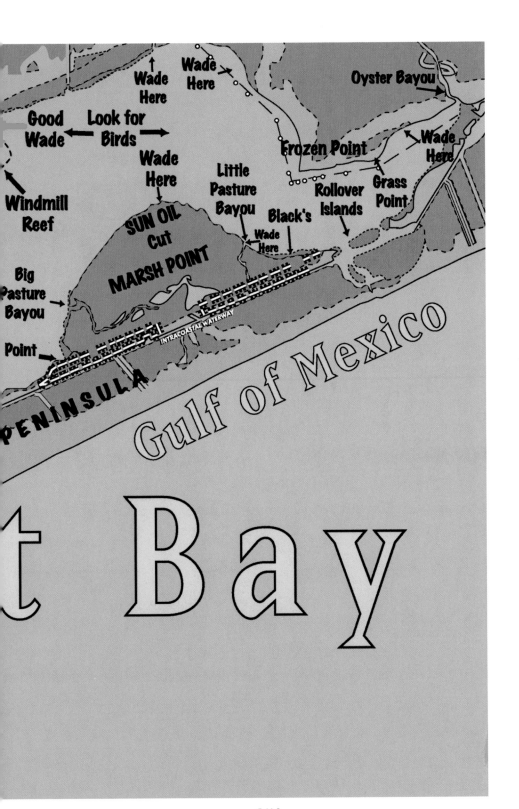

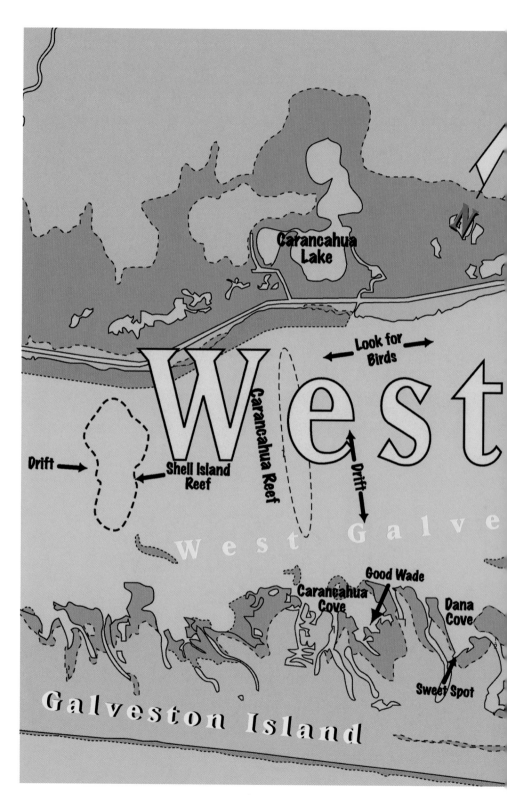

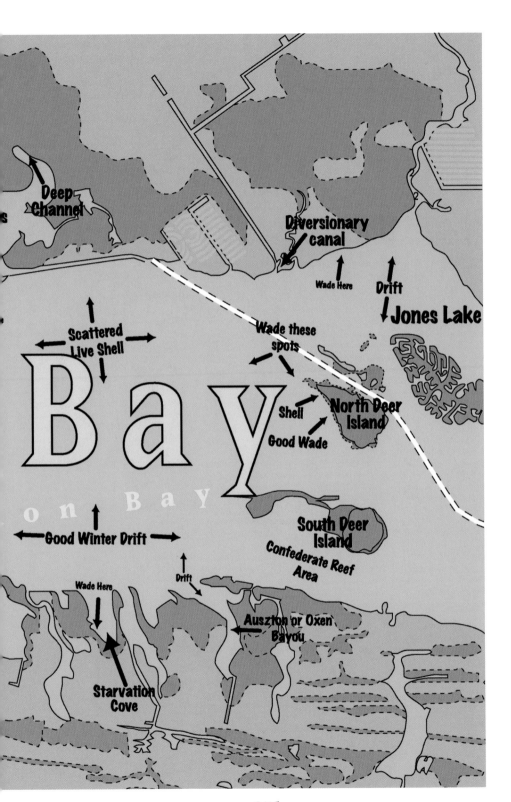

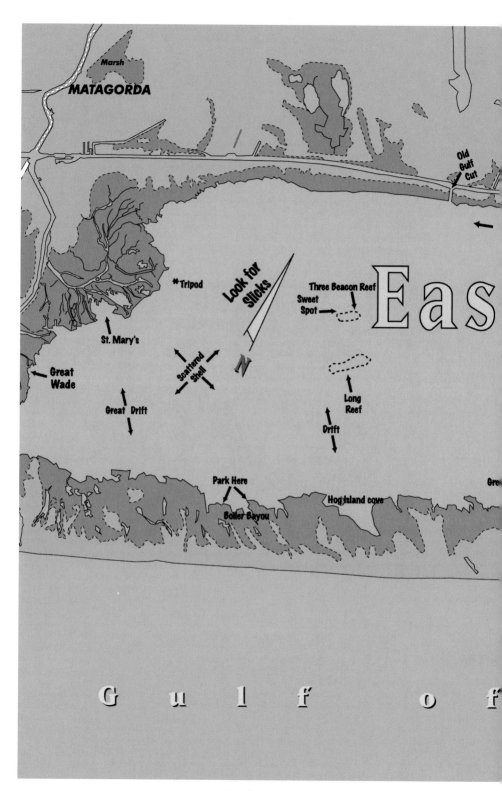

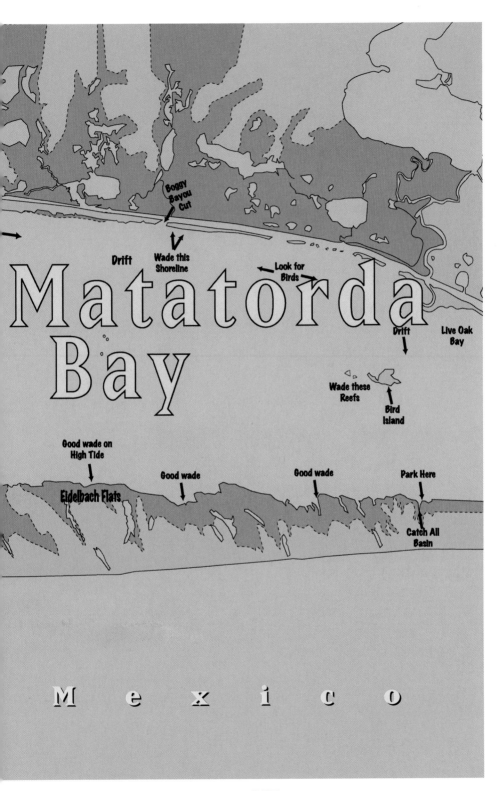

Boggy Bayou Cut

Drift   Wade this Shoreline

Look for Birds

Matatorda Bay

Drift   Live Oak Bay

Wade these Reefs

Bird Island

Good wade on High Tide

Good wade   Good wade   Park Here

Eidelbach Flats

Catch All Basin

M e x i c o

Rocport/Fulton

Aransas

Wade He

Wade Here

Allyns Bight

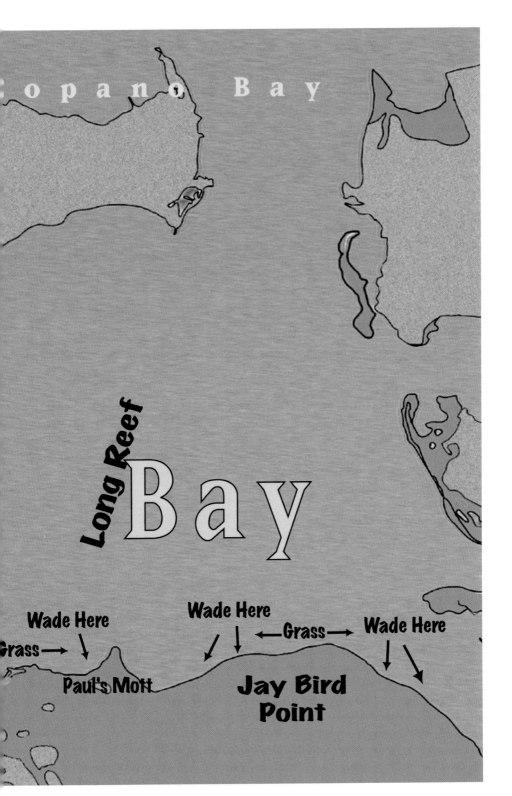

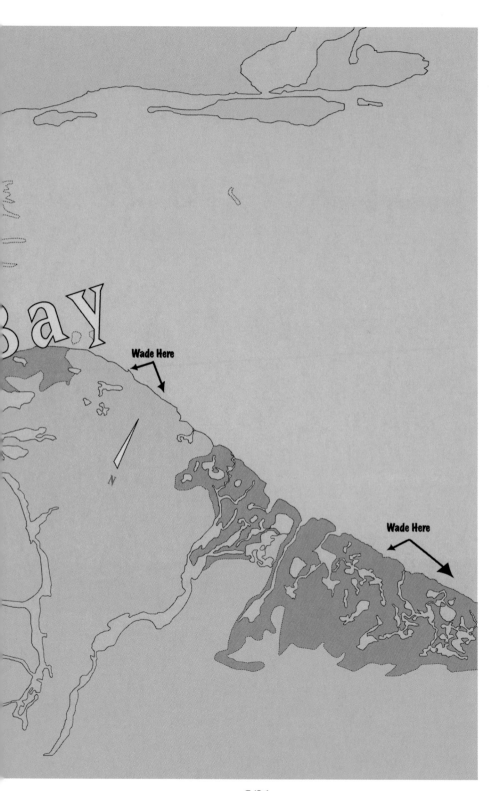

It does not take a big boat to find great fishing along the Texas coast.

ren sand flat that is almost always clear and loaded with mullet and glass minnows. In summer, it is more of a parking lot than a wading flat. The best advice is to fish close to Stingaree Cut. The cut does not receive as much pressure as the flat and has a number of small points along the bank that hold fish.

Fat Rat is usually abandoned throughout fall. After the first solid cold front in October, wait for the wind to turn back to the southeast or south and wade a strong incoming tide. You will likely have the flat to yourself. The topwater action can be great.

Yates Bayou provides several good wading options. Substantial marsh outflow feeds the soft, muddy shoreline on the south bank of the bayou cove. There is a shell point about halfway between Stingaree Cut and the bayou mouth. Try wading that point as you work toward the bayou mouth. This is a classic spot for early spring and fall trout.

The northeast bank has more of a sand base until it leads into the mud at the mouth of Big Pasture Bayou. This is a prime spring wade-fishing spot that can sustain clear water in a northeast, east and southeast wind.

Remember to fish the mouth of Big Pasture. On an outgoing tide, trout often gang up at the bayou outflow. For some reason, these shorelinescan be at their best in the last hours of light, particularly in spring. You can fish all day and see nothing, then the area comes alive just before sunset.

The Sun Oil Cut splits Marsh Point. It has a partial cove at its outflow with a mud and clay base and steep shorelines. It provides a good wade on the east side of the cut on an outgoing tide. In late fall, it is a great spot to fish 51MRCHG MirrOLures and glow Corkys on the fall of a bull tide.

I can honestly say that I have caught more personal limits of trout wading the mouth of Little Pasture Bayou than any other single spot in the bay. It has two shell points to the east that create partial coves. The best approach is to wade the western point and work your way up to the mouth of Little Pasture. On an outgoing tide, stand at the mouth and cast upcurrent with a pearl jerkworm or shad tail on a 1/8-ounce jighead. Let the bait settle in the current. It is a pattern that really works.

Known as Blacks, the stretch of shoreline roughly centered between Little Pasture and the cut into the ICW is a legendary spring and fall big-trout spot. With scattered fingers and spats of shell, this generally muddy bank can provide phenomenal topwater fishing on a strong incoming tide. In times of excessive freshwater inflow, this stretch can become quite salty as strong incoming tides push from Rollover Pass. When a salty tide hits this bank, trout and redfish are quick to follow.

The Rollover Islands stretch across the northern face of the ICW in front of Rollover Pass. They are extremely muddy but have scattered shell reefs that hold trout and lots of redfish. Wade them if you dare, the mud is awful. They can also be drifted with a trolling motor when the wind is light.

The Anahuac Wildlife Refuge occupies the far northeast corner of the bay. With Rollover pass to the south, Oyster Bayou to the east and numerous marsh inflows and bayou tributaries in the area, it is arguably the richest part of East Bay's ecosystem. The shoreline west of Frozen Point can tolerate east, northeast and north winds. The hook of the point will sometimes hold clear water even under a hard springtime east wind. It has some shell and lots of semi-soft mud bottom. In fall, it is full of shrimp, shad, glass minnows and mullet. No wonder the trout and red fishing is so good. Redfish are generally tight to the bank while trout suspended under whatever baitfish are in the area.

Take time to wade the shoreline behind Grass Point. This area is a redfish haven that can produce quick limits as early as late August through as late as December. The key is a high tide and light north or northeast wind.

Windmill Reef is located almost dead-center on the north shoreline. It is easily identified by the lone windmill on the shoreline. The flat directly in front of the windmill is semi-hard sand that tapers to softer silt on the east and west sides. On a high tide, the grass stands against this bank offer great redfish action.

The reef itself is located far off the bank, almost straight out from the windmill. Look for birds working over trout in late spring and early fall. The actual reef has no oyster markers. This is where your PVC manual depthfinder comes into play. Feel around as you learn this reef. Note well any humps or drop-offs.

Moody's Reef is located on the west side of the lone pier pilings on the north shoreline, west of Windmill. The inside of the reef extends to near the shoreline and offers a prime wading spot year-around as the wind allows; north or northwest is best. Moody's actually extends quite a way into the bay. The outer, southern edges are in four- to six-feet of water and present a prime, yet virtually unknown, spot to look for slicks, birds and mud boils.

Deep Reef has it all. It produces limits of trout and redfish and always holds the potential for a trophy fish. It is well-marked by oyster marker sticks and covers a large area. During summer, this reef endures a lot of pressure, but the majority of fishermen crowd the northern end of the reef. Often, the sparsely marked southern tip is left unfished. It is a great spot to look for slicks and mud boils. As with most mid-bay reefs, soft plastic tails are most productive, but Deep Reef can produce fish on topwaters even in five- to six-feet of water.

This is another prime spot to use your PVC pole. Over the years, I found ridges of shell and spots of mud that consistently produced fish even through slow bite periods. Feel around and note what you find. It will pay off.

Richard's Reef is located on the far northwest end of the bay. Sitting just east of Smith Point, it enjoys the outflow of Trinity Bay and the native fish populations of East Bay's north shoreline. During periods of strong freshwater inflow, trout and redfish are pushed around Smith Point and travel across Richard's in their flight from low salinity. The reef is easily waded and tapers far enough into the bay to facilitate drift-fishing on its south end. It is best on a north or northwest wind and is a great late-summer spot.

As popular as Hanna's Reef is, it is amazing how few anglers know how big it is. Most think of its visible hump, Bull Shoals, and neighboring shallow hump, Ladies Pass. The reef extends over acres of bay bottom and actually reaches almost to the south shoreline. It has live and dead parts and provides trout and redfish fishing year-around.

The hump of Bull Shoals can be waded, but be careful when anchoring; a breakaway means a long swim or lonely wait for assistance. The southeastern end of the reef extends almost to Pepper Point and is one of the best reefs for numbers of trout from June through September. The keys are patient drifts through the oyster marker sticks and looking for slicks. Although shrimp under a rattling cork is effective, dark jerkworms and shrimp tails can work wonders.

East Bay's strength comes from its rich marsh and strong Gulf inflow. With neither of these attributes likely to abate soon, I believe East Bay will continue to produce long into the future.

WEST GALVESTON BAY

As many positive words as I have written about Galveston's West Bay, I have never claimed it is pristine. It has had its rough periods, but

I am the first to say it should be declared the Most-Improved-Bay of the 1990s. I see no reason why that improvement will not continue well into the new millennium.

With areas of prolific oyster growth, little commercial shrimping

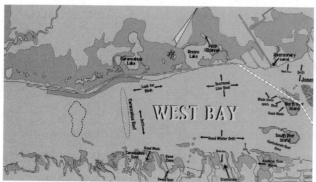

or oystering in the main body of the bay, dramatic wetlands restoration projects, and a tremendous Gulf inflow, West Bay is a great option for trout and redfish anglers.

West Bay Color Map, page C/14

West Bay has historically been thought of as a wintertime bay, but with a little adaptation, local anglers now consistently catch fish year-around even in the looming shadow of Houston's skyline.

The meat of West Bay is in the many nooks and crannies that make up this slender fishery. The first step is understanding the role of Jones, Caranchua and Green's lakes. In a bay that lacks extensive natural marsh, these lakes provide substantial marsh inflow and support a significant portion of the bay's shrimp population. Thus, during spring and fall, these shallow bays become havens for trout and redfish as shrimp stream out of the marsh. The lakes rarely produce large trout but can fill a day with smaller trout and keeper reds. If no birds are working, patient blind drifts often produce prowling redfish.

These lakes can withstand almost all winds without significant muddying. Although they can produce fish on high tides, they are best when the tide has fallen and the majority of the marsh fish have been pushed to the middle of the lake.

My favorite lake wading spot is on the northwest shoreline of Jones Lake, just above the Diversionary Canal. This shoreline has a line of live oyster spats close to the bank and a quick drop-off into a parallel gut. In a north, northwest or calm wind, this shoreline is a sure bet for redfish. Make a long wade, and you will find fish. Try topwaters, but do not make a wade without a 1/4-ounce gold Johnson Sprite spoon; it is a killer. Keep your eyes open for birds working at the mouth of the Diversionary Canal in fall.

North Deer Island is a popular drifting spot among West Bay anglers but receives very little attention from waders. The southeast side of the island produces redfish tight against the bank and has a shell flat on the corner of the bay side of the island that is a great trophy trout spot. A high tide is essential. This shoreline is best in spring and fall.

The southeast end of the island is loaded with oyster shell that creates a series of guts and humps that hug the island. Others run parallel to the old Intracoastal Canal. Some of these reefs are visible, others detectable only with a depthfinder. They provide great drift-fishing in fall and winter for trout and redfish. Try wading the shell ledge on the north side of the old Intracoastal directly between North and South Deer Islands.

The stretch of the old Intracoastal canal that splits the islands is also worth a drift during winter.

Green's Cut is synonymous with West Bay. Like so many legendary spots, the name applies to an immense area. Multiple boats can fish at Green's Cut and never interfere with each other. The general area is between the old Intracoastal to east of Green's Cut then into the new ICW on the north shoreline of the bay. This wide expanse of bay-bottom is covered with live spats of shell and periodic clearings of mud. It is a consistent producer for trout and redfish from Thanksgiving until New Year's Day. Although it holds fish year-around, fall and winter is best.

In the dead of winter, the trick for catching fish here is no trick at all. You simply drift long stretches of clear water. Make long drifts and use your PVC pole to learn the bottom. Although streaky spots can hold numbers of fish, the clear areas tend to hold larger fish and schools of reds. Have your drift marker ready. When you catch a fish, throw your jug. It may mark a big school. Do not be surprised if a school stays in an area for a long time. It is not unusual to come back to the same jug repeatedly and continue to catch fish.

The spoil banks between North Deer Island and Green's Cut offer a fantastic big trout wading opportunity. Shell humps lining the south side of the Intracoastal waterway drop into the canal to the north and into the bay to the south. There are several cuts, including Pat's, Bobby's and Meacom's. These three prominent cuts provide substantial breaks in the shell line and are prime big trout ambush points. Wait for a gushing, incoming tide during fall or winter and try a wade throwing a pearl with chartreuse back Corky. You may catch one for the wall.

The south shoreline coves are being overhauled with new erosion protection, cord grass and sea grass. These improvements will pay great dividends in the future. The coves receive substantial wading pressure in winter, producing good numbers of fish for those willing to grind it out. The keys to success are a high, incoming tide and lots of patience. The bite is often late in the day and sometimes extends into nightfall. The prime coves are Starvation, Dana, Hoeckers, and Carancahua. Most big trout and redfish are caught in the backs of the coves wading bayou inlets and dense mud. It is rarely pretty but can win a lot of local trout tournaments.

Confederate Reef is probably the most misunderstood in West Bay. It is really an intricate string of shell fingers extending from behind South Deer Island. Many of these shell ridges are wadeable and almost the entire area is driftable. Time an assault here to coincide with moving tide (I prefer incoming) and fish the drop-offs of the shell ridges. Wading or drifting, concentrate on finding fish suspended along the ridges. If wind and tide allow, one of the best methods is using a trolling motor to ease along the shell fingers and fish various depths until you find fish. When the tide drops significantly in spring or fall, try drifting in front of Auzston (or Oxen) Bayou where the farthest western stretch of Confederate ends. This shell, sand and mud mix is a great area for redfish pushed from the bayou and nearby coves. It can also produce some large trout (Sorry to give this one up, Leo).

West Bay is no longer out of the question during the heat of summer. The deep shell of Shell Island Reef and Carancahua Reef are good options. Drift in 3-to-5-feet of water over these primarily dead shell reefs and key on slicks.

Shell Island is the best kept secret in West Bay. Most anglers do not know that the island only marks a small hump of the reef, which runs almost as far as Carancahua toward the north shoreline. Patience is critical to finding a summertime bite on these reefs. The hot water bite is often short and the schools of trout and redfish can be very transient. Live shrimp under a rattling cork is the best producer, but light jigheads with jerkworms and shrimp tails can be effective. I have always found a plum with white tail shrimp tail the most effective bait.

For summertime wade-fishing, there are few sites along the entire coast that hold the mystique of San Luis Pass' expansive sandbars. Formed by the rip and flow of Gulf and bay currents see-sawing through the pass, these hard bars create shallow flats set in an entanglement of deep, flowing guts. Wind and tide are the gatekeepers to success on these hallowed flats. The best case is a light incoming tide and equally passive southeast wind. This creates a green surf and pushes rich, emerald water across the bars. Timing is everything, and you never know what your next cast will bring.

Patrolled by big trout, reds and the occasional monster shark, the bars offer adventure waiting to happen. If a strong south or southeast wind ruins the pass, nearby Rooster Collins Flats on the bay side of the western tip of Galveston Island provide a good wind dodge that can produce some formidable topwater action. White topwaters have always been the bait of choice for stalking the bars and flats of "The Pass." Bring some spoons and soft plastics with 1/4- to 3/8-ounce jigheads to probe the deep current of the surrounding guts.

Although not technically part of West Bay, every angler should be familiar with the Campbell's Bayou area. Located on the east side of the Galveston causeway, this western shoreline of Lower Galveston Bay provides a hedge against strong south and southwest winds that often wreck the majority of West Bay. The tip of Virginia Point offers several shell fingers that stretch perpendicular from the curved shoreline. Wade deep to the edges of these shell humps. The fish suspend over the transition from shell to mud. As anglers cover up the northern face of Campbell's, Virginia Point draws surprisingly little traffic. My favorite bait is a glow or pearl with chartreuse back Corky. Work it slow, then slow it down some more.

Galveston's West Bay is easily accessible from I-45 and is surrounded by great facilities and ramps. Its lack of commercial pressure and blooming habitat make it a growing resource for the future.

EAST MATAGORDA BAY

Immense oyster reefs, meadows of matted shoreline grass, acres of pristine marsh, and virtually no industrialization or urbanization make East Matagorda a true jewel in Texas' coastal crown. With freshwater inflow from Caney Creek and some bleed-over from the Colorado River, East Matagorda has become an incredibly strong ecosystem rich with habitat and attendant links of the food chain from microorganism

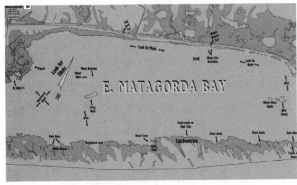

Matagorda Color Map, page C/16

to monster trout.

It was virtually unknown and unfished until increasing pressure from upper-coastal anglers emerged as they migrated to virgin territory. East Matagorda now receives regular fishing pressure but has the resources to support it. What it lacks in Gulf inflow it makes up for with natural estuary. It has outstanding drift-fishing and wade-fishing opportunities for trout and redfish and potential for a trophy-class trout.

The far east end of the bay is characterized by its nutrient-rich mud. Outside of scattered oyster shell reefs and bay-bottom grass, mud is the theme. Thus, it is very susceptible to becoming off-colored in high winds, but the mud and associated structure make it prime ground for big trout and schools of redfish.

The Brown Cedar Cut area is the big trout field. It is difficult to wade many areas surrounding the now-defunct cut, but this rich area has and will continue to produce big fish for those willing to wade with topwaters and Corkys. It is rarely an easy wade but can produce the fish of a lifetime.

The Catch-All Basin is a small nook on the south shoreline. This bayou-fed cove is a prime tournament spot. Depending on the tide level, the main gut that runs through the middle of the basin is prime. On a high tide, the back bayou inlets generally hold more fish. Many anglers think of this area as a wade-only option, but when the tide falls out during fall and winter, drifting the scattered shell knobs out from the cove can be very productive. Fish fall off the shoreline and suspend over the oyster spats.

Oyster Farms is a series of shell piles that extend from roughly the middle of the south shoreline. The reefs themselves are good for wading, but the grassy flats against the south shoreline are incredible. With a series of bayous and distinct meadows of matted sea grass, these flats are worth a look year-around.

The Eidelbach Flats stretch to the west from the Oyster Farms. This relatively flat shoreline is broken up only by periodic cuts and mini-coves. It is best on a high tide when it attracts large schools of trout and redfish tight to the bank. If conditions allow, try working the outside grass line where the grass fades into mud. This structure often becomes a highway for transient schools of trout.

Kain Cove is the McDonald's™ of East Matagorda: Everyone knows how to get there, everyone knows how to drive through it, but only a few get a Happy Meal™. Kain has several large bayou inlets in the back of the cove and a stretch of oyster shell running through the middle of the cove. This combination of structure makes it a prime cove. As Charlie Paradoski once said, "If it wasn't for the crowd, you could catch 'em in there every day." I believe he is right. Like so many of the south shoreline coves, Kain can tolerate a south, southeast, east and even a northeast wind. The grassy eastern shore of the cove is protected even when the rest of the bay is brutalized by wind. Its neighbor, Hog Island Cove, offers equal protection from wind and has ample grass and bayou guts.

Boiler Bayou is another go-to south shoreline spot. The Boiler area is loaded with prime marsh outflow, guts and grass flats to attract fish in all seasons. Key on the far south shoreline windmill to get into the Boiler area and select a fishy-looking bayou cove.

The western bank of East Matagorda is the most underutilized part of the bay. St. Mary's Cove and the numerous unnamed coves to the north and south of it are filled with grass and oyster shell. Almost all have bayou inlets and enjoy very limited bleed-over from the Colorado River. These coves are protected in westerly winds but during cold weather, sustain under surprisingly strong easterly winds.

Shell at the mouths of coves helps keep them fishable. They can be waded or drifted. There is substantial shell extending out from the coves in 4- to 6-foot water that can be some of the best drift-fishing in the bay. The area to the north, marked by the tripod, is a great place to catch limits of trout and has the potential for monster catches of big trout.

Much of the north shoreline is fishable. The prime spots are generally around Old Gulf Cut and Big Boggy Cut. There are many shell humps visible from a passing boat. Most of these humps trail away from the visible structure and offer great wading opportunities. Drifting is also a good option around the cuts. Even in horrible water conditions, birds often work at these cuts in late summer and in fall.

Bird Island is both wade and drift friendly. Shell on the southwest side of the island creates a ledge that can produce substantial stringers. Mud makes the north face of the island cumbersome to wade but can produce big fish for the nimble wader. Drifting the shell humps between Bird Island and Live Oak Bay is a consistent producer of trout during fall. The shell on the east end of the island is always worth a drift.

In the middle of the bay, there is a host of great spots. Three-Beacon Reef and Long Reef are two of my favorites that can both be drifted or waded. The tips of the reefs are the best starting points. I prefer the west ends of the reefs but have found fish on all sides. Remember that Long Reef is true to its name and is a really long reef. You need to thoroughly cover both ends before giving up.

Drull's Lump sits roughly in the middle of the bay above Oyster

Farms. It is an extremely popular spot for good reason. It produces lots of fish and has given up some real trophies. The east end provides the best wade. The general rule is to stand on the end of the shell tip and cast soft plastics out to where the shell tapers into mud. The best drift is focused around the shell ends as well.

Halfmoon Shoal sits roughly between Bird Island and the south shoreline. It follows the same general reef pattern with the tips being the best starting points. I prefer the eastern tip for wading and drifting. In low tide situations, try long drifts all around the outside of the shell. You will be surprised how far the scattered shell extends.

Fishing flocks of birds is an option from late summer through fall and again in spring. Bird fishing is what really put East Matagorda in anglers' sights. With routine keeper trout and occasional 4- or 5-pounders in the mix, no flock should be ignored. The great thing is, when the flocks are really working, you can let your jig sink to the bottom and catch redfish with the same consistency.

East Matagorda is a small bay. Its seemingly unending supply of keeper-trout and trophies does have limits, but it is a viable bay that should continue to produce well into the new century.

Clearly, I have not enumerated every spot (that would be a book by itself), but am confident I divulged enough to ensure receiving hate mail from East Matagorda veterans.

ROCKPORT

Rockport is not really a bay. It is a complex of bays. Maybe I am cheating a bit with this final pick, but if I had to choose only one area to fish (sorry, Galveston), it would be Rockport.

This incredibly diverse complex seems to have it all—miles of pothole-studded grass flats, mid-bay reefs, shoreline shell reefs, incredibly vibrant surf, and a seemingly endless supply of spots to fish. It has

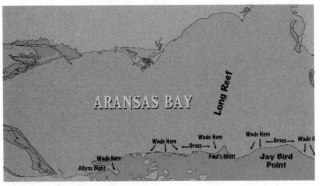

Aransas Color Map, page C/18

some freshwater inflow, abundant sea grass, live oyster shell, and a strong bay ecosystem and food chain.

Rockport has become a very popular fishing destination over the past decade. The area hosts guides, tournaments and everyday anglers in scores. It receives a lot of pressure, but I believe the lack of urbanization and strength of its habitat make it a viable choice for years to come.

Mesquite Bay is the jewel of the Rockport area. It boasts shell, grass, mud, sand flats, and a slight Gulf influence from Cedar Bayou. Granted, Cedar Bayou is essentially sealed until the next hurricane blows it clean, but high winds and waters from a Gulf low pressure system occasionally pushes ocean water into the bay. In periods of heavy freshwater runoff, it receives critically important inflow and balances this with a healthy estuary structure of cord grass and mud flats.

When the surf is green and flat, there is no finer spot along the entire Gulf coast than Cedar Bayou. It is one of the best spots for a morning or afternoon surf session.

From the closed mouth of the bayou to the shrimp boat wreck that sits roughly 1/4 mile to the west is the hotspot. This area has distinct bars with sharp drops into soft guts. The topwater action is unbelievable, and there is always a chance to see a rolling tarpon. Try chrome or bone Ghosts and Super Spooks and do not forget to bring a spread of 51M series MirrOLures (CHG, HP and 51).

The best perk in the Cedar Bayou surf is the chance to catch

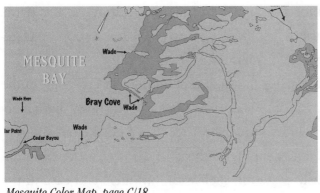

Mesquite Color Map, page C/18

numbers of slot-sized redfish on jigs. When the top-water bite abates, try slow-jigging a red shad or pumpkinseed Bass Assassin in the guts. You may find a surprising number of redfish. The surf is accessible through the bayou with a shallow-draft boat. Although you cannot go all the way into the surf by boat, you can anchor and hike a short distance to the beach. The next closest access is through the Aransas Pass jetties.

On the bay side of the Cedar Bayou cut is the Cedar Bayou flats. This semi-soft bay-bottom is covered with scattered shell and matted grass. With a mix of nearby Gulf influence and estuary-like habitat, it screams "Big Trout Here." The flat gradually drops into the bay and is bordered by harder sand on the west end of the shoreline. The water is generally murky due to the soft bay bottom and provides top-tier-spawning grounds for trout.

Longtime Rockport angler Robby Byers is a regular to this area and champions the value of slicks.

"With often off colored water, you have to key on slicks to find the fish on this flat," Byers said. "I generally throw a bone Ghost or a plum swimming shad on a 1/16-ounce jighead. Both baits are effective in low-visibility conditions. A 1/4- or 1/2-ounce weedless gold spoon is not a bad call for redfish."

The Cedar Bayou flats are best waded, but if the crowd allows, they can be drifted. Focus drifts on mullet movement and slicks. Experiment throwing topwaters out of the boat; you may find a school and want to hop in for a wade. One of the best features of this flat is that it is not necessarily a first-morning-stop place. It can support a late-day bite, even in the heat of summer.

Byers regularly stalks the shell reef on the western point of the entrance into Cedar Bayou. "There is a distinct shell ridge that tapers into deep water and sand bottom," he said. "It is a good trout and red-fish spot that can tolerate a south, southeast and, at times, even a south-west wind." Cautiously wade the shell with topwaters and ease to the edge to fish the drop-off with jigs.

Mesquite Bay offers so much prime wade-fishing that it is hard to narrow it to a few spots. The shoreline east of Cedar Bayou has a series of reefs just off the bank that offer great wade-fishing, particular-ly during the low tides of winter. As redfish and trout are pushed out of the marsh, back lakes and off shorelines, they school around the deep-er structure.

The prime spots are where reef tapers into bay mud. Try wading the length of the reef but focus on the tip. Dark jigs are generally the best call. On a low tide, look for the reef tops and anchor in the mud outside of the reef. This allows you to thoroughly fish the area sur-rounding the reef.

It is impossible to dissect the Rockport area without mentioning the south shoreline of Aransas Bay. From Spalding Cove to Long Reef and down to Allyn's Bight, this shoreline is a model for seascape artists. It is impossible to guess how many paintings these flowing grass flats have inspired—or how many trout and redfish have been caught there.

The Fence Lake shoreline (so named because it sits directly out from the lake) is located roughly between Long Reef and Allyn's Bight. It has abundant grass with fairly deep potholes. The shoreline tapers steeply into mud.

During spring and summer, the outside grass line holds schools of smaller trout. Although not all are keeper-sized fish, there is a lot of potential to cull out a limit. Dark jerkworms on 1/16-ounce jigheads are the best call. The inside of the shoreline is dotted with distinct potholes that hold roaming packs of redfish and occasional large trout. Try a bone- or Halloween-colored Ghost for probing the potholes.

The shoreline between Spalding Cove and Long Reef offers a similar stretch of grass but with fewer potholes. This shoreline almost always has some schools of reds on it. It is often a matter of wading far enough to find them. I am not a big believer in leap-frogging a wade, but by dropping one or more waders off, then anchoring several hundred yards down the shoreline, you can cover this expansive shoreline and locate the largest concentration of fish.

To cover a lot of water, use a bone or Halloween Ghost. If you are getting near-miss strikes, switch to a plum (dirty water) or clear-glitter (clear water) shad tail on a 1/16-ounce jighead. Although you will likely snag some grass, try dropping the shad tail into the potholes and use a straight retrieve with little jigging. The swimming tail is sufficient to elicit strikes. During the heat of a summer afternoon or sustained southwest wind, floating grass can clutter this shoreline and make fishing a frustrating experience. Try a weedless spoon, but in extreme situations, even this is small help.

Byers believes that the Spalding-Long reef shoreline is an all-day producer much of the time. "Like the Cedar Bayou Flats, you do not have to fish this shoreline at the crack of dawn. To be honest, my best catches have come through mid-morning and even the afternoon," he said. "The grass line on the drop-off of the shoreline is a decent mid-day trout spot as well. There are often a lot of smaller fish, but there can be plenty of decent-sized fish as well." As on the Fence Lake shoreline, Byers prefers a dark jerkworm on a 1/16-ounce jighead.

Spalding Reef runs parallel to the south shoreline roughly

between Spalding Cove and Jaybird Point. It is within eyeshot of the shoreline and marked only by a few PVC pipes. A long stretch of the reef is exposed and clearly visible during low tide.

Like several reefs in Aransas Bay, Spalding is a great wading reef. It sports several shell points and fingers that meander off the spine of the reef and supports a healthy trout population through spring, summer and fall. The water around the reef can become muddy with sustained winds, but do not let that discourage you. Try loud, white topwaters and dark soft plastics to combat dirty water conditions.

To the north of Mesquite Bay looms San Antonio Bay, a large, open bay with the same familiar grass shorelines and defined shell structure of its brethren bays.

The south shoreline between the second chain of islands and Panther Point is a legendary spring and summer wade-fishing hotspot. With areas of dense grass and potholes, it supports a large trout and redfish population. In a south or southeast wind, this shoreline is crystal clear; its grass can maintain water clarity in some surprisingly adverse wind.

Part of what makes San Antonio bay so rich is the availability of freshwater inflow. During periods of extreme flooding, it can become very off-colored. Chicken Foot Reef sits almost directly north of this shoreline. This diverse shell complex offers great wade-fishing and is a prime area for free-lining live croakers for trout.

The Rockport area is a saltwater angler's dreamland that literally has it all. From habitat to fish populations, Rockport just instills a sense of confidence on every wade or drift. It is a place where you can always feel like the next cast will produce a fish, maybe even a trophy.

Chapter
Fourteen

Hiring a Guide:
An ex-guide's perspective on hiring a pro

Countless articles have been written concerning the proper protocol for hiring a guide. Having spent a number of years as a professional guide on the Texas Gulf coast, I believe I can cut to the chase.

During an early-morning coffee session, David Wright gave the best description of a guide's task I have ever heard: "To consistently catch fish with customers, you have to put people on a lot of fish that are feeding very aggressively." Sounds easy. To catch fish with all levels of anglers, Capt. Wright's assessment is true. Some clients are looking for more than just fish from a guide, but the majority just want to catch fish, a lot of them and preferably big ones.

To get the most out of a guided trip, try to make your guide understand that you want the whole experience, not just a box full of fish. At first, your guide will not believe you. I never did. But as you show yourself to be a conscientious angler who honestly wants to improve his skills, a good guide will be happy to help you.

PHOTO BY PAT MURRAY

No guide can guarantee stringers like this every day.

It is amazing how a no-pressure trip puts a guide at ease and actually makes him more proficient. My best trips usually came with regular clients. Part of that can be attributed to their skill and expertise, but a repeat customer allows the guide to relax and think clearly. In this scenario, the guide can be more experimental and will usually produce more fish and a better learning experience. As stated in the Introduction of this book, no one can guarantee anything more on a fishing trip than sunrise and sunset. The fishing is a constant, the catching a variable.

CHOOSING THE RIGHT GUIDE

There are maybe a dozen guides that I would book—but that does not mean there are only a dozen good guides. It means there are only a dozen guides I know of that fit my style of fishing and needs on a trip. Selecting a guide entails more than simply randomly picking one from the classifieds in the back of a fishing magazine. Each guide has his own particular style of fishing, his own strengths and weaknesses. Some are wade-fishing specialists, others will not get out of the boat if $100 bills are floating on the water. Some excel at drift-fishing, some at live bait fishing. As you can see, just any old guide will not do. Angler and guide must mesh to ensure a pleasant, rewarding experience.

The best way to find out if a guide is right for you is a simple conversation. Call some of the names you commonly hear about from friends and read about in articles, and feel them out. Never believe the hype. Make your own assessments based on how your inquiries are answered.

Go to wintertime fishing trade shows and visit the booths. If a guide is at a summer show, he or she is likely not booked or has an obligation to a sponsor. The winter shows are the time to get an accurate feel for a guide's demeanor. While there, attend as many seminars as you can. You will be able to see the guide in action. A guide's attitude on stage will likely mirror his style on the water. Seminars provide a great testing ground for a future trip.

It is important for a guide to be full-time, but if he is not, it should not be a deal-breaker. Desire and knowledge can make up for a deficit in daily experience. The advantage of fishing with a full-timer is that he is constantly racking up more time and experience on the bay and, more importantly, is seeing patterns emerge and dissolve on a daily basis. A full-time guide knows what is a two-fish spot or a 20-fish spot from day-to-day.

Never lie to yourself or your guide about what you want out of a trip. If you are more comfortable fishing with live bait, you better tell your guide, or you will be dissatisfied and your guide frustrated. Ask your guide what style of fishing he likes and ask for a recap of the past season. This brief snapshot will allow the guide to give you a picture of the pattern that typifies a trip.

You Have Hired a Guide—Now what?

Once you have found the right guide, make sure you go with the right group of anglers. The wrong group with the right guide can still end in disaster. Make sure that the anglers accompanying you on the trip expect the same thing you do. If you combine two die-hard drift-fishermen with a die-hard wader, someone will feel cheated and the guide will feel torn. If you want to learn spots and could care less about catching fish, make sure your fellow investors are on the same page.

If you have the right guide and the right group of anglers, try to book one trip every season. When split among three anglers, the cost is affordable for the value you get. You almost have to think of your trips as investments. Like a quarterly draft that is drawn from your checking account for a retirement account, your quarterly trip is preparing you for the future of your fishing (try explaining that one to your spouse). If you book one trip every season for several years with a good guide, you will see multiple bays in different conditions. You will learn multiple patterns, many of which can be applied throughout the year.

A good guide is like a set of Cliff's Notes for the Texas bay system. A guide can provide an instant education that will jump-start your knowledge of a bay. If you are new to an area, a guide can eliminate months or years of trial and error and teach you to assess a bay like an expert. Most competent guides fish multiple bays and bay systems, giving you the opportunity to broaden your horizons and skills.

Ask Questions

Most guides enjoy teaching. They would not be in the business if they did not. Guides who simply want to catch fish and become "guides" to finance their passion quickly become disgusted with clients and, subsequently, the whole business. For a guide to make it, he or she must like people and enjoy helping them learn to catch fish. Most successful guides fit this mold. When you ask questions, you allow the

guide to speak on a subject that is dear to a pro's heart.

Bring your own GPS unit on your trip. Most guides will allow you to use a GPS to mark productive spots. The thing to note is that the spots do not make the fisherman. Your guide knows well that it is the knowledge of patterns and techniques combined with specific spots that make an angler. Your guide should

The author and longtime friend Phil Cambra – note the ugly boat in the background.

have no problem with you bringing a GPS to build your library of key spots. If he objects, think twice about booking.

After the trip, make notes when you get home. Draw drift patterns and wade tracks on your maps. Create pictures of surface and subsurface structure that were important to your trip and to catching fish. Note every place your guide took you. If you did not catch anything in a spot, ask why you fished that spot. The subsequent story will likely give you the confidence to return to the spot.

If you decide to take up a new style of fishing such as tarpon fishing or fly fishing, a guide can help you assess the necessary equipment and skills. Before you jump head-first into something new, see how a pro does it. It will save you time and money.

Chapter
Fifteen

Tips from the Pros:
If I could only have five lures...

Growing up in and around the Galveston Bay area, I dreamed in saltwater hues. Fishing was literally everything to me, and not surprisingly, fishermen were my heroes. Not firemen, policemen or baseball players, but fishermen. If they had saltwater angler trading cards, I would have been a collector. How much do you think a Rudy Grigar rookie card would be worth today? Although now written in jest, at that time, I was that serious.

As I built my interest and subsequent tackle collection, I always wanted to know what baits the coastal pros and legends used. Even if I was not in the right spot at the right time, I would at least have the right bait. There is some rationale to this thinking. If you have confidence in the bait you are throwing, you have isolated one of the variables for success. With this thought in mind, I asked several coastal legends and pros what baits they would carry if they could only have five. They had to be specific in style, brand and color. Although not listed in order of importance to them, each bait selection took careful thought. Believe me, these guys labored to whittle their arsenal down to five selections.

Without slighting anyone, I chose two coastal legends (Pete Tanner and Leon Napoli), an innovative lure maker (Paul Brown), a well-traveled outdoor writer (Doug Pike), and two veteran coastal guides (Mickey Eastman and James Plaag). This diverse group's selections represent a wide assortment of baits and reflect the factors that motivate their fishing. From pure leisure to business, there is a clear agenda behind which five lures they would choose.

PETE TANNER

Mr. Tanner has seen and fished it all. He is a walking, talking coastal legend. From the Texas redfish wars of the 1970s to his present-day exploits in his brand new 22-foot Pathfinder, he is a well-seasoned coastal angler. Mr. Tanner fishes purely for leisure and does it with great regularity. His picks:

Corky slow-sink model in pearl with chartreuse back.

Corky Devil in pearl with chartreuse back.

MirrOLure Top Dog Jr. with white belly, clear sides
and chartreuse back.

Heddon Super Spook with orange belly, gold sides
and black back.

Shrimp tail in strawberry with a white tail.

LEON NAPOLI

Leon's success on the Troutmasters' circuit only further substantiates his years of experience and expertise on the coast. With roots dating back to commercial rod-and-reel fishing in the early 1970s, Leon now fishes purely for pleasure and is an avid, successful tournament angler. His picks:

Bass Assassin in red shad.

MirrOLure 51MR28.

Half-ounce gold Johnson Sprite spoon.

Ghost topwater in glow (white).

Corky with pink back, silver sides and pink belly.

PAUL BROWN

Paul is the inventor of the Corky. Although he will deny owner-ship of any of his many baits, Paul is the master of coastal lure making. He humbly defers all credit to his brain trust of legends and pros, but I do not care what he says—he is the inventor. His picks:

Corky slow-sink in clear-silver flake with chartreuse tail.

Corky slow-sink in glow (chartreuse).

Corky Devil in pearl with a chartreuse back.

Super Devil in pearl with a chartreuse back.

Heddon Super Spook with white belly, clear sides and chartreuse back. (Paul admits modifying the colors a little. How surprising of a lure inventor.)

DOUG PIKE

Doug is a true multi-media outdoors communicator. He writes for magazines and newspapers, edits a major national conservation magazine, and hosts a radio show. When Doug goes fishing, he may be on a jetty in Port Mansfield or drifting a reef on Sabine Lake. His lure picks reflect his eclectic approach to coastal fishing:

Heddon Super Spook Jr. in black & gold.

A 1/4-ounce weedless Johnson Sprite spoon in gold.

MirrOLure Top Dog Jr. in black.

Norton Sand Eel in avocado with chartreuse tail.

DOA Baitbuster in natural mullet.

MICKEY EASTMAN

Mickey is one of the original full-time, professional fishing guides on the upper Texas coast. His fishing career has been heralded in countless magazine, newspaper and radio testimonies. Mickey founded the Troutmasters Tournament series. His name is synonymous with coastal bay fishing. His picks:

Bass Assassin in red shad.

MirrOLure Top Dog Jr. in black.

MirrOLure Top Dog Jr. in Fire Tiger.

Heddon Super Spook in Chrome with a blue back.

Corky slow-sink in clear glitter with chartreuse tail.

JAMES PLAAG

James is another pioneer guide. He has nurtured his guiding operation through many bays and beachfronts to build Silver King Adventures. He has won numerous categories and an overall championship in the CCA Texas Guide's Cup Tournament and recently won Pro-of-the-Year in the Troutmasters series. His picks:

Bass Assassin in limetreuse.

MirrOLure 51MRCHG.

MirrOLure She Dog in chartreuse and silver.

A 1/4-ounce gold spoon.

Corky slow-sink in glow (chartreuse).

This is merely a snapshot of these great anglers' tackle boxes. There are dozens of other equally qualified legends and pros who have altogether different picks. Although providing a solid starting point, these five bait selections are not silver bullets. They are simply a few pieces in one big picture, but it is nice to see what others put their money on when things get tough.

Chapter
Sixteen

Tournament Trout Tactics:
Techniques and philosophies for winning
a trout tournament

There is nothing like a tournament to sharpen your physical and mental fishing skills. Beyond the normal uncertainties and difficulties of catching fish on an ordinary weekend, a trout tournament adds an entirely different set of hurdles to a day of fishing. Expert competition, adverse weather and pressure can wreck the most airtight pattern. You have to think on your feet and be physically and mentally prepared to fish every minute of the tournament in top form.

If you look at coastal trout tournament standings, the same names always appear at the top. Some of this consistency can be accounted for by natural ability, but the anglers who consistently win are often the most focused. They meticulously map their strategy, carefully pre-fish and never give up.

I have fished a variety of tournaments over the years, some serious, some not so serious, but in every situation, I showed up to win. Often I did not, but it was never from lack of effort. Every time you fish a tournament it is an opportunity to take your fishing to the next level. Fish every tournament you can. During a tournament, you will get the

opportunity to observe and talk with other fishermen. Just through association, you will pick up valuable insights on winning patterns, why the fish bite or do not, and what winners do to win. A good tournament will make you a better fisherman.

I have compiled several tips for better tournament fishing. They represent some factors that have helped me. There are countless other approaches and philosophies for success. Like the styles of consistent hitters in professional baseball, there are a thousand different warm ups, stances and

Capt. George Knighten savors a large Rockport trout.

swings—and almost all are based in some part on the style of hitters that preceded them. Watch and study proven anglers' performances and refine your style accordingly. To become one of the greats, emulate the greats.

TOURNAMENTS ARE WON FISHING, NOT RUNNING A BOAT

Unless you actually have a pattern that involves fishing spots that are far apart, a running boat is a catalyst for failure. Every second your boat is running, you are not fishing. If you are looking for spots, you are either in such good shape that you are trying something off-the-wall, or you are in such bad shape that you are panicking.

Tournaments are won fishing, not driving. Stick to your pattern, and keep your bait in the water.

USE YOUR EYES

Do not forget to look for fish-signs. Do not get in such a hurry to get to "the spot" that you ignore a slick, mud boil or any other signs. A tournament can be won in one drift or wade. Never ignore the fundamentals of fishing, particularly during a tournament.

This is most true when you are in an unfamiliar bay. If you see something that looks good, fish it. You may find a spot that even the locals do not know.

STICK WITH A FEW BAITS

Stick with your go-to baits. Do not find yourself panicking and constantly changing baits. Sensibly trying different styles and colors of baits can be crucial for getting bites, but maniacally trying to find "the bait" often gets you farther away from what works rather than closer to it. Stick with what works for you.

YOU ONLY NEED A FEW BITES

I have always grappled with this concept. Most trout tournaments only require a few trout for a complete creel. I have always pursued numbers of fish and have had to break myself of the inclination to go for numbers. Create a game plan that centers on quality, not quantity. Fish areas where you have caught heavy fish in the past or spots that are known to produce good fish. These areas are known for big fish for a reason.

On the other side of this idea, remember that you are not looking for a string of 7-pound trout. Do not try to knock the ball out of the park. If you can catch 3- and 4-pound trout in every Troutmasters tournament, you will finish in the top ten in the majority of tournaments.

EVERY TOURNAMENT CAN BE WON FROM THE BOAT

Granted, not every tournament will be won while drift-fishing, but I firmly believe that every trout tournament, regardless of location, can be won drift-fishing. Even in Rockport and Baffin Bay, drifters catch large, tournament-class trout and often do not have to deal with the shoreline crowds.

The majority of tournament fishermen are going to run to their favorite shoreline spot and ignore the middle of the bay. It is the rebel minority that sometimes wins the tournament.

It is axiomatic that large crowds on a shoreline can push shallow fish into deeper water. Use this to your advantage. For example, the wading crowd on East Matagorda bay can push fish off the grass lines to deeper, shell-studded structure. By drifting the outer reaches of the shoreline that are beyond a wader's reach, you can target fish that have fallen off the shoreline pattern.

Big trout do not live exclusively on shorelines. There are times when not only a few big fish but most of the big fish are in the middle of the bay. Do not try to fight the trend. If the fish are in the middle of the bay, go to them. Wade-fishing will always be part of a winning pattern, but do not exclude drift-fishing in your game plan.

TAKE THE ROAD LESS TRAVELED

Tournaments are often won in unlikely spots. Primetime spots are often worked over by pre-fishing and tournament crowds. By working one or two unusual spots into your tournament pattern, you increase your chances of fishing a virgin school.

Although there are times when you have to join the crowd to catch fish, tournaments are usually won by the oddball pattern

GRIND, GRIND, GRIND, AND GRIND SOME MORE

There is a real estate adage that the three key selling features for real estate are location, location and location. Many fishermen mistake this as a fishing adage. They spend so much time trying to find the right location that they forget to fish. The anglers who win tournaments are grinders.

Veteran tournament angler Leon Napoli once pointed out to me that if you find a spot where you can catch a 4-pound trout during pre-fishing, you have a very likely tournament spot. His logic is sound. Usually, if there is one 4-pounder in an area, there are a few more and the possibility of a really big one. If you catch a 7-pounder, it is likely a loner. Conversely, a 2-pounder is usually accompanied by a school of 2-pounders. Find a spot that has the potential to produce 4-pound fish, and grind it out.

DO NOT LET CROWDS OR WEATHER
PSYCHE YOU OUT

There are two things synonymous with tournaments: big crowds and bad weather. Even if the weather reduces the crowd, the remaining anglers are generally clumped into a few fishable areas. This can be overwhelming, but remember that bad weather is a good thing for a tournament. It reduces the competition and crashes game plans. Unless it is you who has been whacking 5- and 6-pound trout prior to the tournament, a big wind is a great equalizer. Use it to your advantage. For those of us who cannot pre-fish, a big weather change is a blessing.

Do not let another angler or anglers covering up "your spot" ruin your tournament. Try to stay calm and think clearly. See if you can comfortably fish the area as well. If not, move to your "B" spot or try to anticipate where the crowd may push the fish. Do not linger and watch another angler catch your fish. That will only ruin your concentration and waste your time. If someone beat you to your spot, move on and look at it later.

NEVER GIVE UP

Tournaments are won in minutes. You win a Troutmasters tournament with six casts. There are other tournaments and divisions within tournaments that can be won with a single cast. The big trout for a tournament could be caught on your first or last cast of the day. Never give up. Even if your game plan exploded in the first day or hour of the tournament, keep grinding. It is extremely hard to put together one solid day of fishing, not to mention two days. If you struggle on the first day of a two-day tournament, the first-day leaders may struggle on the second.

Reevaluate your game plan. If it is solid, run with it. If you feel it is no longer valid, recalculate a plan and fish it as though it was the first day of the tournament. You may be pleasantly surprised with the results.

A CLOSING THOUGHT

I have always admired the focus and intensity of tournament bass anglers. The successful ones literally live the experience. I cannot suggest that trout tournaments have evolved to that level—frankly, it is unlikely they ever will—but they have awakened a competitive spirit in saltwater trout fishermen that was not evident in the past. Even if they do not win, the anglers who compete and fish hard become better fisher-men with every tourna-ment.

When you com-pete against yourself and your own circle of friends, you limit your scope. When you compete against the general public, you stand to raise your goals and improve your fishing skills.

The Troutmasters and a host of other tour-naments spawned in the '90s have done a great ser-vice to the bays and the anglers who fish them. The proposition of com-

David Wright with a classic East Bay stringer...WOW.

petition has wakened some great anglers who had grown tired of the weekend boat ramp rat-race, spurring them back into the game with new fervor.

Tournaments have recruited new anglers into the game and, thus, added longevity to the sport. Some would question the conserva-tion ethic in tournaments that put additional pressure on the resource and lead to greater harvest of large fish. I have to disagree. I do not fear anyone catching all the fish. I fear no one caring about the fish. If recre-ational anglers are not involved in the fishery, the resource has lost its best advocate.

Tournaments promote the sport and serve as one of the few recruiting tools for the sport of fishing. Tournaments elevate the sport. They are typified by small creels and altruistic fishermen. They not only sharpen the fishing skills of anglers, they help recruit conservationists.

Chapter Seventeen

Conservation:
Conserving Texas' Coastal Resources

"Conservation" is a word that should be more than dear to every angler's heart. It should be a part of their everyday life and, definitely, a part of their outdoor ethic. Fishing without participating in the efforts of conservation is equivalent to checking out books from the library and never returning them. As anglers, we accept an unwritten obligation to help conserve the resource not only for our continued enjoyment, but also for future generations.

STEWARDSHIP

In thinking of each individual's role in coastal conservation, I like the word "stewardship." We are stewards of Texas' rich coastal resources. That is a role not to be taken lightly. Part of it entails making sure state and federal fisheries managers do not arbitrarily partition off large areas of bay and ocean waters into "no-fishing zones" without first exhausting all traditionally effective fisheries management methods. The balance to avoiding draconian closures is to equally ensure that our fisheries are not over-utilized to the point of destruction. The very definition of conservation, "the wise use of natural resources," embodies this principle.

We are very blessed in Texas. Our fisheries are in surprisingly good shape. Having seen the impact of weak management and severe commercial overfishing along our sister states' coasts, I can say that Texas is ahead of the fisheries management curve, but that is no reason to let the conservation line go slack.

Involvement is implicit to good stewardship (and I do not just mean going fishing). Without proactive involvement by recreational anglers, it is probable that we would not enjoy the robust fisheries that Texans currently has. Did commercial gill-netters police themselves in the name of stewardship? For that matter, did state and federal fisheries managers guarantee the health and longevity of our coastal waters? Recreational anglers have always been the driving force that changed the tide of fisheries management, and guaranteed a future for our bays and nearshore waters.

This spirit of involvement gave rise to the Gulf Coast Conservation Association (GCCA), now the Coastal Conservation Association (CCA), and arguably the birth of modern marine conservation. CCA ushered in a true spirit of stewardship that values marine fisheries in a broader light than merely price-per-pound. Prior to the organized involvement of recreational anglers, the rebuilding and restoration of marine fisheries was virtually unheard of. Now recreational anglers and CCA set the standard for marine conservation throughout all coastal states and beyond.

WHAT IS CCA?

In 1976, 14 concerned recreational anglers gathered in a Houston-area tackle shop to discuss the overfishing of redfish and speckled trout in local Texas bays. When redfish carcasses began to outnumber spawners, these recreational anglers organized, focused their efforts, and pushed for positive change. They raised awareness, involvement, and—most importantly—money to make a difference. They pushed for change on all levels, especially in the legislative arena. CCA founders eventually banned gill nets, established game fish status for speckled trout and redfish, and blazed a path for better conservation in Texas that we enjoy today. It is probable that without recreational anglers organizing and creating CCA, there would be few (if any) redfish along the Texas or Louisiana coasts, or possibly any state along the Gulf Coast and beyond. Between gill-netters, purse-seiners, and a cadre of blackened redfish-crazed Louisiana chefs, all could easily have been lost. The spirit of altruism that typifies recreational anglers made the difference.

Remarkably, CCA functions with the same positive impact now

as it did then. With different battles that are arguably more complicated than the early redfish wars, now tens of thousand of recreational anglers make up the body of CCA Texas membership and conservation strength. The now-famous "Save the Redfish" campaign has broadened in scope to encompass such issues as ensuring sufficient freshwater inflows into Texas bays and estuaries, proper management of coastal commercial shrimping and crabbing practices, funding critical marine fisheries studies programs, supporting pro-resource legislation and regulation, and a seemingly unending list of other conservation-related programs, projects, and initiatives. There is no doubt that CCA and its army of volunteers and supporters cannot do it all, but the tradition in conservation that started more than a quarter of a century ago with CCA still rings clear in current Texas conservation efforts.

THE ESSENCE OF CONSERVATION

The spirit of conservation must continue if the resource is to be properly maintained. It is actually surprising that our bays and nearshore waters are as robust as they presently are, even with current conservation measures. A client solidified this thought for me many years ago at the conclusion of a rather mediocre guided trip. With only a few trout caught during the trip, I mentioned my regret for the slow bite and expressed whatever excuse I had for the day (no tide or bad moon phase always sounds good). One of the anglers who had little experience on the bay looked at me in amazement and said innocently: "Slow trip? I am amazed that we can catch anything out here. With all of these shrimpers, crabbers, oystermen, and fishermen, it is a wonder that a redfish, crab, or even a jellyfish survives." He had a point. For an outsider looking into the daily activity on the bay, it could look like some third-world lagoon where every edible scrap is extracted from the bay until it is barren. Yet, even with this pressure, the bay continues to produce. It is incredibly resilient, usually finding a way to repair itself if we apply the proper conservation measures to let it.

This is where every angler comes into the picture. Through getting involved in the conservation of Texas marine resources, every angler can make a difference. Involvement comes in many forms. Catch-and-release fishing is one of the most obvious. Clearly, catch-and-release is great, and there is no doubt that a little voluntary restraint goes a long way to conserve our fisheries—but it is not enough.

Recreational anglers have to get involved in conservation on a deeper level to truly make a difference. This ethic does not necessarily manifest itself in the tedium of attending public hearings and submitting testimony on issues of passion. Stewardship is reflected in being aware of the issues facing our bays and being involved with a proactive group or association that enacts positive change. No one group is perfect (although I have my prejudices about CCA), but there are a variety of fisheries conservation and advocacy groups from which to choose.

In the early 1980s, David Cummins (now National President of CCA) was volunteering at a Houston-area boat show, signing up new members for GCCA. He tells the story of an angler wandering by the booth and, after being asked to join, the angler said: "I will join when you get nets out of the water." Can you imagine where our bays and estuaries would be now if CCA's founders thought that way? What if they waited for someone or some group to fix the problem?

Just as in those early days of conservation, recreational anglers must give their time, effort, and dollars to shape the future of marine conservation. Not everyone is meant to give the countless hours that some do in the name of conservation, but most can give support by joining a credible conservation group, staying aware of the issues, and practicing sound conservation in their own outdoor activities.

We have a lot to be proud of in Texas. Our tradition in conservation is a road map and beacon of hope for states that do not have some of the most fundamental conservation laws in place. It is incredible to think that gill netting is still a regular practice in many coastal states, even along the Gulf Coast, but we cannot ever let complacency undo all that has been gained.

Conservation is not a given in any state. We must remember that we are the stewards of the bay, and our work for proper conservation is our payback to the coast for all of the enjoyment it provides us.

Chapter Eighteen

GPS:
A global perspective

Lowrance 256-color LMS-335C DF combination 50/200 kHz fishfinder and GPS+WAAS chart recorder

As I have written, said and preached, GPS numbers and the spots they mark are not the alpha or omega of being a better fishermen. They are possible locations, nothing more. Remember that your GPS is not going to locate fish, your senses and skills are.

These numbers are an addendum to the map section of this book. I have selected a few choice spots and some prime general locations for drifting and wading that will put you in the position to be a more consistently successful angler. Take these locations and build on them. Use them as signposts to direct you on the correct road. They will not ensure a successful trip—you have to do that.

SABINE LAKE

Coffee Ground Cove: N29 57.74 W93 45.58
Coffee Ground Cut: N29 58.56 W93 46.37
Stewts Island Area: N29 54.349 W93 53.030
Southern Lake Reef Drift: N29 47.06 W93 54.94
Greens Bayou Area Drift: N29 49.44 W93 49.92

GALVESTON EAST BAY

Fat Rat Area: N29 28.55 W94 38.83
Hanna Reef Area: N29 28.617 W94 44.671
(remember this is a very large reef)
Deep Reef Area: N29 30.80 W94 40.58 (very large area of shell)
Richards Reef: N29 31.40 W94 44.28
Robinson Bayou Area: N29 34.26 W94 34.24

GALVESTON WEST BAY

Jones Lake Area: N29 17.83 W94 56.24
(mostly shell and prime for drifting)

Confederate Reef Area: N29 15.81 W94 55.30

Western Greens Cut Area: N 29 15.26 W94 59.02

Carancahua Reef Area: N29 12.84 W95 00.25

Shell Island Area Drift: N29 12.13 W95 01.08

EAST MATAGORDA BAY

Halfmoon Reef Area: N28 43.33 W95 46.30

Eidelbach Flats Area: N28 41.25 W95 49.03

Boiler Bayou Area: N28 38.77 W95 53.075

Long Reef Area Drift: N28 40.25 W95 53.30

West End Area Drift: N28 40.28 W95 56.03
(look for slicks and birds)

ROCKPORT

Jaybird Area: N28 05.18 W96 55.71 (look for bait)

Paul's Motte Area: N28 03.166 W96 56.395

Fence Lake Shoreline Area: N28 00.60 W96 58.43
(look for mullet and slicks)

Cedar Bayou Area: N28 07.16 W96 49.85

Brays Cove Area: N28 08.52 W96 48.61

Try these numbers, but treat them as ingredients in a recipe. Just like a good cook, you should have lots of "ingredients" for improvisation and experimentation. For more GPS locations, check out *Texas Fish & Game's* annual *Texas Lakes and Bays Fishing Atlas*. The writers and editors of that edition painstakingly recorded a host of new and old GPS numbers for bays up and down the coast. There are also a growing number of reliable maps available that note GPS numbers for every imaginable drop of water on the Texas coast.

Saltwater Glossary

Fishing Terms:
From "bay rage" to "zero"
a listing of basic and often
humorous insider terms

bay rage. *An act of extreme anger and disgust directed at an angler who has interfered with another angler's fishing pattern. Can equally occur at a boat ramp when one boater is annoyed at another boater's lack of boat-dock acumen.*

bigtime, big-time. *An event or activity that is going or went very well.*

black-soling. *The act of making annoying black marks on white fiberglass with black-soled shoes. It is a matter of courtesy to never wear black-soled shoes aboard a white fiberglass boat.*

blow-up. *(1) A fish striking a surface plug, generally associated with a missed strike. (2) The destruction of any mechanical device, from a fishing reel to an outboard engine.*

bug. *A live shrimp.*

'cane. *Short for hurricane, but can refer to any large storm.*

croaker soaker. *One who fishes with live croaker.*

fishery. *All fishing activities directed toward a given species or species complex.*

flapper. *A fly fisherman.*

free-lining. *Fishing live bait with only a hook for terminal tackle, thus allowing the bait to swim freely.*

green trout. *Freshwater large-mouth bass.*

grind. *To expend extraordinary effort and time to catch a limited number of fish.*

grinder. *One who grinds, usually a compliment.*

hopper. *A live shrimp, often a large white shrimp. See bug.*

hot. *A shark.*

hot wagon. *A shrimp boat, so named for attracting sharks.*

how 'bout 'cha. *(1) Phrase used to hail another VHF marine radio user. (2) An exclamation. e.g. Upon seeing a 9-pound trout one might exclaim, "How 'bout 'cha!"*

loom. *Derogatory term for a johnboat or aluminum boat that has just ruined your fishing pattern. Coined by James Plaag in Upper Trinity Bay.*

lurker. *An angler who follows another boat to the point of stalking. See potlicker.*

mauler. *Mansfield Mauler. A popping cork on a piece of wire with swivels at each end and affixed with rattling beads.*

mud boil. *A small cloud of mud stirred up by a bottom-feeding species such as redfish and black drum.*

mud hole. *A place unsuitable for fishing, particularly a wind-torn bay or flat.*

nasty. *An unpleasant person, place or circumstance.*

pelagic. *A fish species normally found in the open ocean, often beyond the continental shelf.*

pencil. *An undersized or very thin speckled trout.*

plug. *(1) A hard-bodied fishing lure. (2) A boat's drain plug.*

potlicker. *A derogatory term to describe an angler who unabashedly follows other anglers to find a pattern.*

Rambo. *The act of plowing at great velocity into a flock of feeding gulls and terns or a surface-feeding school of redfish. Can be complimentary or derogatory depending on the situation.*

slick. *A bloom of oil on the water's surface caused by the oily regurgitation of fish.*

struggler. *One who struggles to catch fish with regularity. Coined by Jim Leavelle: "Never underestimate the heart of a struggler."*

track. *A path or pattern of slicks or mud boils.*

train lights. *Four or more 250-watt bulbs mounted in a box that is affixed to a telescoping stand and powered by a portable generator. Used to attract baitfish and hence game fish when fishing at night.*

turbid, turbidity. *Water colored or "stained" by silt or mud stirred by wave action.*

zero. *Term to describe a bad catch or bad fisherman, as opposed to "hero."*

Index

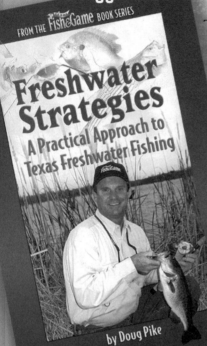